SOME EDIBLE MUSHROOMS
AND HOW TO COOK THEM

SOME

EDIBLE

MUSHROOMS

Portland · Oregon · 1964

AND HOW TO COOK THEM

By
Nina Lane Faubion

Edited by
L. K. Phillips

BINFORDS & MORT, *Publishers*

SOME EDIBLE MUSHROOMS
AND HOW TO COOK THEM

Library of Congress
Catalog Card Number 62-15309
Second Edition

CONTENTS

Introduction   vii

Part I—Mushrooms with Gills

Amanitas   12
Parasol Mushrooms   22
Meadow Mushrooms   32
Inky Caps   46
Milk Mushrooms   60
Wood Growing Mushrooms   62
Chanterelles   70
Tricholomas   72

Part II—Mushrooms without Gills

Puffballs   78
Sponge Mushrooms, the True Morels   94
False Morels   100
Coral and Club Mushrooms   110
Pore Mushrooms   120
Spine Mushrooms   140

Part III—Mushrooms as Food

Selection and Preparation   161
Special Recipes   164
General Recipes   170
Mushrooms, a Survival Food   186

Mushrooms in Color   144
Glossary   190
Index   195

Mushroom species vary widely in shape, size, color, and edibility:

And with age or stage of development:

Pennsylvania State University

INTRODUCTION

This enlarged and revised second edition of *Some Edible Mushrooms* stems from the wide acceptance and continued demand for the popular earlier edition. As with the original edition, the purpose of the present one is to acquaint the amateur mushroom hunter with a number of the common yet delectable mushrooms, and to point out characteristics of the few poisonous ones.

Collecting is limitless because mushrooms grow in almost every locality throughout the world, and approximately ninety-eight per cent of them are edible. They thrive wherever there is moisture along with decaying leaves or logs.

The term "mushroom" goes back to many countries and many tongues, back to Anglo-Saxon and Dutch and German; to Icelandic, Danish, Russian, and Scottish and French; and of course back to Latin. In Latin, *muscus* means a mossy place, a bog, a morass, or a swamp,; especially a peat bog, as on the Scottish border. In the French there is *mousse* for "moss"; and their word for the small white mushrooms—like those of the fairy-ring—is *mousseron*.

Mushrooms have been used as table foods for two thousand years; they were a delicacy at the feasts of the Caesars. Epicurean tastes in all times have elevated the plants to high places; they invite gormandizing. However, by the exercise of reasonable care, they are easily digestible and contain highly beneficial food values.

"Going mushrooming" in the soft, gentle showers of spring and fall reaps rich rewards for recreation and appetite. Careful attention to these pages of text and illustrations will enable many persons to add to their variety of foods and immeasurably increase the pleasure of a jaunt into the woods and fields. Interest and activities in out-of-door life are taking more and more people into the open; it is a useful discipline to train one's powers of observation and learn their dependability.

Nearly ninety species of mushrooms are here described and illustrated; and their habits, season of growth and use are discussed so that the beginner can learn to identify the parts of the mushroom such as the cap, gills, pores, peridium, ring, stalk, cup or volva, and the veil. By using the Glossary at the end of the book, he can readily understand the exact meaning of these words. He can also learn where and when to look for the different edible species and how to avoid the poisonous or undesirable species.

This book is based on knowledge gained through many years of study and observation of mushrooms. It is purposely simplified in its terminology and avoids many needlessly scientific descriptions. The beginner will be safeguarded if he is guided by the information in this volume, provided he confines himself to the varieties he learns to know and recognize as edible mushrooms. Both line drawings and photographs aid in this identification. However, since this is basically a field guide, not a definitive treatise, neither the publishers nor the author accepts responsibility for undesirable results.

It is necessary for clearness that technical or scientific names be used to positively identify one plant from another. These scientific names are divided into at least two parts: a genus or surname, and a species or given (or first) name. For example, the genus *Lycoperdon* refers to a puffball mushroom, but *Lycoperdon glabellum* refers specifically to the smooth puffball. This identification cannot be accomplished by using only common names as there are at least three genera called puffballs: the *Lycoperdon*, the *Bovistella*, and the *Calvatia*. Besides, many mushrooms are so rare, or have created interest so recently, that their common names are not widely used.

Guide to parts of mushrooms

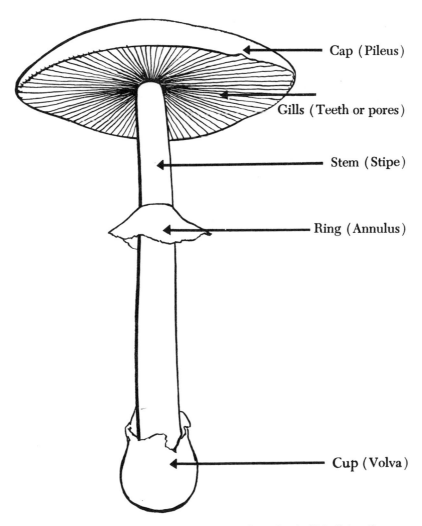

Cap (Pileus)

Gills (Teeth or pores)

Stem (Stipe)

Ring (Annulus)

Cup (Volva)

Pennsylvania State University

According to recent authorities, there is no known final rule for separating the edible from the poisonous mushrooms, and the genus *Amanita* is considered to be the only fatal one. Other species can cause great discomfort—according to the sensitivity or allergies of the user—but in moderate quantities are considered safe.

It is quite likely that many so-called mushroom poisonings have been the result of gormandizing. Like most foods, mushrooms should be eaten in moderation. In spite of all precautions, if you feel you have eaten a poisonous mushroom, empty the stomach and intestines at once, and get a doctor as soon as possible.

The experienced mushroom hunter can take many chances that are not recommended for the novice. The best rule for the novice to follow is: learn to recognize specific edible species by their physical character; be especially cautious and avoid all mushrooms that have any of the danger signals. The beginner can gradually enlarge the number of species with which he is familiar—and so expand his mushroom menus.

No one should hesitate to collect mushrooms. The different species, especially the more common ones, can be identified as easily as the various vegetables and fruits in the markets, the flowers in the garden, or the trees in the forest. During the course of a year, in an average yard, six to ten different species, described in the pages of this book, will be found growing. Some of these, including the Fairy-Ring, are among the best flavored of the mushrooms.

Mushrooms can be prepared in many ways. They are delicious stewed, baked, broiled, or used fresh in salads or as seasoning. They may also be dried or frozen. Their abundance throughout the woods and meadows, from the seacoast to the mountains, makes them a sought-after food for survival.

In mushroom hunting, one wonderful trip into the meadow or woods, plus one dish of delectable mushrooms, will add another collector to the enthusiastic thousands who have had this experience.

In her Preface to the original edition, the author states:

"I personally learned a great deal about mushrooms as a young girl at the heels of my father, as my sister and I followed him through the woods, over the fields and meadows, and into the glens, gathering and classifying mushrooms—known and unknown to science. Later, at home, my mother prepared and cooked the specimens and we ate them—unknown ones rather timidly, it must be admitted—with father's medicine chest open and apothecary scales ready for service.

"In this way, father (a noted mycologist) discovered and classified several important varieties, heretofore unknown or unrecorded. Some of those we discovered on our jaunts now appear in highly recognized scientific volumes. For years we ate and enjoyed mushrooms that afterwards we found had been previously classified as poisonous. But at this writing many that were classified as deadly have been officially cleared and given a safe bill of health.

"In this volume are many of the tasty recipes that I enjoyed as a child and have continued to enjoy through the years."

Part I—Mushrooms with Gills

AMANITAS (*Amanita*)

To start the amateur properly I shall introduce him to the poisonous mushrooms, and afterward lead him along pleasanter paths in this country of the fungi with its colorful and mysterious riches.

The beginner should never eat any of the Amanitas. This group of mushrooms is found over the North American continent generally and, as far as I personally know, seven varieties occur in the Northwest. The family is not a large one; not more than thirty complete the membership of this deadly circle. A most careful study of all their botanic points should be the duty of the person who sets out to gather mushrooms. Learn the death signals, as you do your traffic laws. So far as is known, no other species of mushrooms contains the fatal poisons.

Yet the Amanitas are classed as the aristocrats of all fungi. Their beauty of structure and coloring and their noble bearing set them apart. This very beauty tempts the novice to swoop upon his woodland find, but from the moment he touches the fungus, he is inviting death.

While several species of Amanitas are edible, for the beginner all shall be classed as poisonous, just by way of precaution. By this I mean that the danger signs will be dwelt upon at some length, so that an Amanita will be recognized as an Amanita, regardless of its edibility. I ate some of them once, but they were gathered by an old Italian woman who was familiar with her Amanitas. I would not eat one that I had gathered myself. I do not trust myself that far with them. Of those growing so luxuriantly on the Pacific Slope, only one of the edible varieties is common.

Death Cup
Amanita phalloides
Poisonous

Fly Amanita   *USDA Photo*
Amanita muscaria
Poisonous

Pennsylvania State University

Development of Amanita, showing
progressive formation of cup and ring.

All Amanitas grow upon the ground. They seldom grow in open fields. Their chief habitat is in woods, groves, margins of woods, and land recently cleared of trees. They spring from a universal veil, which at first covers the entire plant. As the plant grows it bursts this veil, usually carrying the upper part on the umbrella-like cap, the pileus, where it appears as patches or warts or scales, the remainder enclosing the stem at the base as a volva or cup. This volva is white and is either a cup-like form, or a series of partial rings, or it is a sheath quite readily crumbled or pulverized. The entire plant should always be dug up, to examine for the presence of a cup.

There is also a partial veil in the early stages of growth, which extends from the stem to the margin of the cap, enclosing the gills. When ruptured, this partial veil extends from the stem as a ring. The gills of the plant are free from the stem. The stem is white and has a white ring, that which has been left from the broken partial veil. The spores are white.

The spores are the small, dust-like reproductive bodies of mushrooms; the mushroom itself is called the fruiting body. In the gill mushrooms, like the Amanitas, the spores are produced on radiating blades of tissues, or gills, on the under surface of the cap. Sometimes it is necessary to extract the spores from the gills to identify the species.

Spores may be white (as in Amanitas), black, or a variety of colors, according to species. To make a spore print, remove the cap of the mushroom close to the stem. Lay the cap, gill side down, on a piece of white paper. Cover the mushroom cap for an hour or two. The spore print will appear as a fine powder arranged in the same radiating lines as the pattern of the gills themselves.

When the Amanita is young, its ovate or button-like form is often mistaken for the common Field or Meadow Mushroom, even by experienced mycologists. The novice should never gather the buttons before they have developed so that the gills can be seen. The gills of the Amanita are white; while those of the

Meadow Mushroom are pink, their gills later becoming blackish-brown.

There is no necessity for detailed classifications here. The only necessary things for the novice to learn—and those most thoroughly—are that the Amanita is a poisonous mushroom; and in gathering mushrooms in the woods or on the borders of woodlands, he should look well for the danger signals flaunted by all members of this family.

Grandmothers' poison tests are not to be relied upon. A silver spoon does not turn black when cooked with the Amanita; neither does milk curdle when the Amanita is boiled in it—and, contrary to legend, most of the poisonous mushrooms peel beautifully.

If one is timid about eating any of the various mushrooms, the best way to test them is to eat a very, very small piece of the variety chosen, and if no discomfort results, enlarge the sample until quite sure that the variety is not harmful. Each individual is constituted differently, and one man's meat is another's poison. The only mushrooms that I bar are those of the Amanita family. For years I have eaten mushrooms that have been labeled poisonous, just as many others have done, and I have found them not only edible but delicious.

The aim of the novice in regard to the Amanita should be, first, to recognize the enemy, and second, to destroy it. He will never be harmed by this species if he obeys instructions and refrains from gathering gilled mushrooms in the woods. It is in order, therefore, to give brief descriptions of a few of the most common of the Amanitas.

Of the genus *Amanita,* one of the most highly poisonous species is *A. phalloides,* which follows. This is the Deadly Amanita or Death Cup, recognized by the presence of a cup at the base of the stem. It is sometimes referred to as the Death Angel.

DEATH CUP
Amanita phalloides

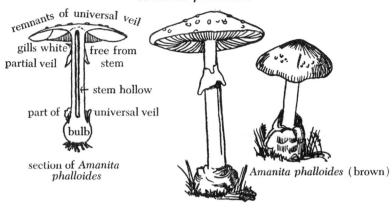

section of *Amanita phalloides*

Amanita phalloides (brown)

Amanita phalloides (white)

Description: The cap is three to four inches broad; commonly shining white or a light lemon-yellow; occasionally olive-brown; fleshy, oval bell-shaped, then expanded—completely spread out. It is covered with thin skin, which is not sticky, yet it clings to the fingers in wet weather. The cap is naked, rarely sprinkled with one or two fragments of the volva. The regular margin of the cap is even.

Stem is three to five inches long, one-half inch or more thick, bulbous, narrowing upward. It is hollow, rather smooth and white. The ring, above the middle of the stem, is slightly marked with lines, swollen, commonly entire and white.

The volva, or cup, is more or less buried in the soil, bulbous, semi-free, bursting open in a torn manner at the apex, with a limber border. The gills are free from the stem, and swollen in the middle; the lines broad and shining white. The spores are white and the odor is rather disagreeable.

Where and When to Find It: The Death Cup grows in the woods on the ground, in margins of woodlands, and lands recently cleared of trees. It is general over the country and most abundant from August to November.

Comment: *Poisonous.* The Death Cup contains the poison, phallin, and is almost invariably fatal when eaten. *Amanita phalloides* closely resembles *Amanita virosa* (also poisonous), but in the *virosa* the top coloring is rarely yellow, and the fetid odor is more marked.

Another species of Amanita that is similar to the *phalloides* is the *Amanita mappa*. This poisonous mushroom is lemon-yellow, becoming green, and has a pronounced stinking odor.

FLY AMANITA
Amanita muscaria

Full-grown
FLY AMANITA

Description: In the Northwest there are two types of *Amanita muscaria.* In the eastern states, there seems to be but one. On the Pacific Slope we have the European Amanita, which is of a deep-red color—maroon, or mahogany—as well as the variety that is a rich red in the center of the cap, shading to deep orange, and into the lighter yellows, until near the edge of the cap where it is a rich cream color. In appearance it looks like a beautiful confection.

The following description applies to both types of *Amanita muscaria:*

The cap is four inches or more broad, normally at first blood-red, soon orange and becoming pale, whitening when old; globe-shaped, then convex and at length flattened; slightly slimy when young; covered with a skin which is at first thick, and in wet weather, glutinous, but which gradually disappears. It is sprinkled with thick, wart-like fragments of the volva. The margin, when full-grown, is slightly furrowed. The flesh is white.

The stem is up to eight inches long; shining white; firm; torn into scales; at first stuffed with limber, spider-web fibrils, soon hollow. The base of the volva is closely attached to the stem, forming an ovate bulb, which has a distinct margin with a series of scales. The ring is very soft, even, and inserted at the apex of the stem—which is often dilated. The gills are free from the stem, but reach the stem, and run down in the form of lines; they are white, rarely becoming yellow. The spores are white.

Where and When to Find It: The Fly Amanita grows in the woods on the ground. Sometimes it is found at the edge of forests; occasionally in brush close to an open field. It occurs from spring through fall.

Comment: *Poisonous.* The Fly Amanita *(A. muscaria)* and the Death Cup *(A. phalloides)* cause most of the cases of mushroom poisoning. The Fly Amanita is so-called because some believe that a mixture made from it will kill flies. Another very poisonous Amanita is the *A. verna,* or Destroying Angel. Unlike the Death Cup, this is always pure white and quite large, ranging up to ten inches in stem length, with a cap that often reaches ten inches in diameter. The Destroying Angel has all the warning signals: white cap, white flesh, white gills, white stem, white spores, and—a ring and a cup.

See color photograph 1.

Fly Amanitas showing the warty cap
and a cross-section of the stem and cap.

OTHER VARIETIES OF THE FLY AMANITA
(*all poisonous*)

Variety *regalis*. Much larger. Stem, stuffed; solid when young; as much as one to two inches thick, becoming light yellow within; the volva terminates in eight to ten concentric rows of small scales. Top, very glutinous; bay-brown, or the color of cooked liver. Gills, yellowish. Grows in the woods, on the ground. Most often found in the fall after the rains begin.

Variety *formosa*. Top, at first lemon-yellow; with mealy, limber, yellowish easily separating warts; often naked. Gills, often becoming yellow. Grows in the woods, on the ground. Most abundant in late spring.

Variety *umbrina*. Thinner and more slender. Stem, hollow, often twisted; bulb narrowed. Top, at first reddish-brown, then leaden colored, with the exception of the disk, which is dingy-brown. Gills are white. The plant is five to eight inches high and grows in the woods. Abundant in late spring and again after fall rains begin.

In popular usage, poisonous mushrooms are often called

toadstools, but whether they are called Amanitas or toadstools is not important to the beginner. What he must know are the physical characteristics which tell him what to look for—and to look out for.

To readily recognize—and avoid—the Amanitas, study the following danger signals:

1. Warts or scaly patches on the cap
2. White to pallid gills, not attached to the stem
3. The stem cleanly separable from the tissue of the cap
4. A ring near the top of the stem
5. A volva or cup at the base of the stem

Note the volva, or cup, of each of the following species of Amanita, described in the preceding pages:

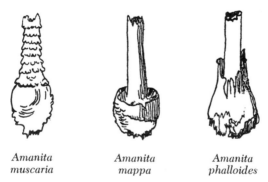

| Amanita | Amanita | Amanita |
| muscaria | mappa | phalloides |

It is reassuring for the casual collector—who is just looking for a pleasant outing and the chance to pick up some choice seasoning for his evening meal—to realize that almost all (98 per cent) of the various kinds of wild mushrooms are edible. Many are not only edible—they are delicious. A number of tasty species have found favor with the most fastidious gourmets from early Roman times to the present. Although the Common Meadow Mushroom is the only one raised on a large scale for marketing in the United States, in Europe more than fifty species are generally marketed.

PARASOL MUSHROOMS *(Lepiota)*

Because of their flat, expanded cap, this group of gilled mushrooms, the Lepiotas, is sometimes called the Parasol Mushroom, or the Umbrella. It is one of the most common mushrooms growing in fields and pastures of the Pacific Slope. Wheat fields are often dotted with species of this genus following the first rains. From late June until after frost, members of the Lepiota family can be found in quantities sufficient to supply the demands of the average family. They are an excellent mushroom for the pot-hunter.

In gathering Lepiotas, the beginner should *never* gather anything that even looks like them in the woods. He should stay in the fields and pastures because there is danger of confusing them with the deadly Amanitas, which grow in the woods and along the borders of woodlands.

Lepiota naucina, commonly called the White Lepiota, bears a closer resemblance to *Amanita phalloides*—in its white form— than does any other, except that the Amanita is seldom found in the fields, and the Lepiota is seldom found in the woods.

The bulb of the Lepiota is continuous with the stem, each passing into the other imperceptibly. The Lepiota has no universal veil so there is no volva or cup. In *Amanita phalloides,* the joining of the stem and bulb is abrupt and remains so, and the bulb is more or less wrapped in the volva or cup. The ring is also larger than in the Lepiota and hangs downward, and the gills are permanently white.

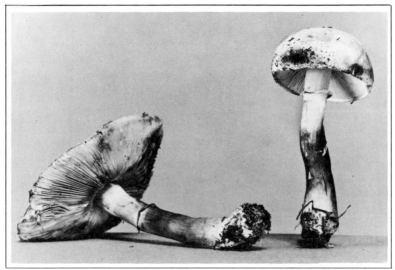

Above: *Below:*

White Lepiota   **Parasol Mushroom**
Lepiota naucina   *Lepiota procera*
Edible   Edible

Lepiota procera (edible)
showing cross-section and "parasol"

American Lepiota
Lepiota americana
Edible

Below:

Green-Gilled Lepiota
Lepiota molybdites
Poisonous

USDA Photo

USDA Photo

Note the structural differences between the Amanita and the Lepiota in the following drawings:

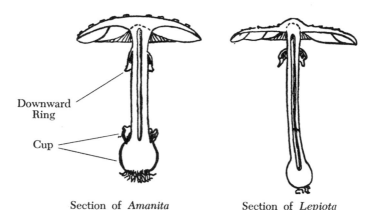

Downward
Ring

Cup

Section of *Amanita*   Section of *Lepiota*

WHITE LEPIOTA
Lepiota naucina

Description: The White Lepiota is soft, smooth and white or snowy-white, as its name suggests. It is ovate when young and usually from one and a half, to five inches across when full grown. In the smaller members of this family, the caps remain smooth, but the larger ones frequently become rough, or minutely cracked in the center. The color sometimes varies from white, to ivory-white, deepening in color at the summit. In a rare form

WHITE LETIOTA
Lepiota naucina

it is scaly; large, thick scales occur which are caused by the breaking up of the cap surface.

Unlike the gills of the *Amanita phalloides*—in its white form—the gills of the White Lepiota change with age to a dirty pinkish-brown, or a smoky-brown color. They are free from the stem, as can be seen in the illustration of the cross section.

The stem is ringed, slightly thickened at the base, and colored like the cap. The outer edge of the veil, or ring, is thickest. Usually the ring is firmly attached to the stem, but movable rings are often seen. As the plant grows older, the ring is often missing, but traces of it can always be seen on the stem. The stem usually tapers upward from a more or less enlarged base. When fully grown, it is hollow, but before that it contains cottony fibres within the cavity or appears solid. In the Willamette valley of Oregon, the stem grows from two to six inches high, although elsewhere it seldom reaches this height.

Where and When to Find It: The White Lepiota grows plentifully in all parts of the country. It is found in wheat fields, pastures, lawns, and by the roadsides, and is also found in the woods, but the warning of earlier pages is repeated. In woods it is best for the novice to leave it alone. In its younger state, it too closely resembles the Destroying Angel for comfort.

Comment: *Edible.* The White Lepiota is one of the best of the edible mushrooms, and—if he will be careful—it is safe for the novice to gather, but he must gather the whole plant. If it has warts on the cap and a cup at the bottom of the stem, it is likely one of the poisonous Amanitas. The White Lepiota has neither warts nor cup.

Another certain means of distinguishing between the two is by toasting a piece of both. The gills of the Amanita will remain white, while those of the Lepiota will turn brown.

See color photograph 3.

Parasol Mushroom
Lepiota procera

Description: The Parasol Lepiota is easily distinguished by its extremely tall stem, shaggy cap—with a distinct knob-like middle (umbo)—and the space between the gills and stem. Aside from its general structure it does not resemble any poisonous species. The caps, from three to six inches across, vary in shades of brown, sometimes having a faint tint of violet. They are at first egg-shaped (ovate), but finally expanded, the skin soon breaking up into brown scales, except upon the very top, which remains smooth. The flesh, while not very thick, is permanently white—like the Amanita—and soft.

The gills of the plant do not reach the stem, and become narrower as they grow toward it. They are of a whitish color. The stem is usually tall and very slender; at first stuffed with light fibrous threads (fibrils), quite bulbous at the base; generally spotted or scaly with snake-like markings below the ring; five to twelve inches high and about one-half inch thick. The ring is thick, firm, and easily moved. When the stem is removed from the top, it leaves a deep cavity, or socket, extending nearly to the outside skin. The spore print is white.

Where and When to Find It: The Parasol Mushroom is often found in quantity in thin woodlands and brushy areas. It occurs from midsummer into the fall.

Comment: *Edible.* Cooked properly, it is one of the most delectable of mushrooms; excellent when fried in butter, and as the base of a delicious catsup. It is widely sought by all mushroom connoisseurs.

See color photograph 4.

American Lepiota
Lepiota americana

Description: The American Lepiota is nearly as common as is the White Lepiota. It has one character in which it differs from all other species of Lepiota. The whole plant when fresh is white except the center of the top, and the reddish-brown scales of the cap. In drying, it turns a dull smoky-red color. The white form of the *Amanita phalloides* does not; nor does the *Amanita verna.* Nor do these Amanitas have the reddish or reddish-brown scales.

In the very young plant the cap is somewhat egg-shaped and nearly covered by the thin reddish-brown cuticle, but as the plant grows the cuticle separates and forms the scales that adorn the cap. In the center of the cap it usually remains entire. The edge of the cap is thin, and usually marked with short radiating lines. The caps vary in width, from one to six inches.

The gills are free and do not quite reach the stem—just as in the White Lepiota. Sometimes the gills are connected with each other at or near the inner extremity by transverse branches. They are a little broader near the margin of the cap than at their inner extremity. Gills and spore print are white.

The stem, from three to five inches long, is somewhat thickened at, or a little above the base; it is white, hollow, and bears a ring. The stem tapers toward the top. The ring is sometimes thin, and disappears with age. Wounds or bruises usually assume a reddish hue.

Where and When to Find It: American Lepiotas grow singly or in tufts on grassy ground, on decaying tree trunks, and on the ground beside them. They may be found from late June until frost.

Comment: *Edible.* This species when cooked is almost as delicious as *L. procera.* It is best fried or broiled, but very acceptable stewed. In stewing, it imparts a reddish color to the liquid in which it is cooked. The caps are meaty and of excellent flavor. Scales should be removed before cooking the caps.

Green-Gilled Lepiota
Lepiota molybdites

Description: The Green-Gilled Lepiota is one of the largest and handsomest of the genus, but should be avoided by the novice, as it is poisonous to some. It is easily distinguishable from edible Lepiotas by the green gills of maturity and the thicker, more club-shaped stem. It sometimes grows to more than twelve inches across, though usually it is only five to nine inches broad, and from six to eight inches high. Whenever there is plenty of rainfall it flourishes, though not in as great an abundance as the White Lepiota.

The cap is fleshy, soft, at first nearly spherical, then expanded, and sometimes depressed — the central part sunken below the margin. It is white, with a brownish or yellowish cuticle that breaks up into scales except on the disk. The gills are close, oblong, and gradually tapering toward the outer extremity. The gills are white until the cap is almost opened, by which time the green spores begin to cause the gills to change to green.

The stem is firm, usually tapering upward, smooth, stuffed, and whitish in color, tinged with brown. It has a rather large movable ring. The flesh of both the cap and the stem is white, changing to reddish, and then to yellowish when cut or bruised.

Where and When to Find It: The Green-Gilled Lepiota grows in pastures and fields, and sometimes in the woods. The novice is again warned about gathering the Lepiota of the woods. Often in the pastures, this mushroom grows in grand fairy rings, from five to fifteen feet in diameter. It is white and noble in appearance.

Comment: *Poisonous.* Because the Green-Gilled Mushroom seems to contain a poison that is harmful to some people, it is generally classified as poisonous. However, it is harmless to others. As some persons cannot eat strawberries, and others cannot eat shell-fish without distressing results, so it is with this Lepiota. Probably fewer persons would become ill from eating it than from eating shell-fish, but the amateur had better not take a chance because the poisoning can be acute.

Personally, I find this a most delicious mushroom. The meat is fine and usually free from worms.

MEADOW MUSHROOMS *(Agaricus)*

The Common Meadow, or Field, Mushroom and several related species are all good to eat, but as some of them are found in the woods, and in the early stages of development can be confused with young or Button Amanitas, the beginning pothunter is again warned against gathering mushrooms in the woods, or along the edges of woodlands. He should keep to the fields and pastures, and not gather buttons until they show signs of color on the gills.

Three types of *Agaricus* flourish in the Pacific Northwest: those with gills very soon pink or of a rose color; those with gills at first brownish or of a delicate gray, and those with gills at first white or whitish.

The drawing below shows four stages of growth in the Meadow Mushroom. Note how the emerging cap is discarding the partial veil in the third stage, and how the remnants of the veil remain as a ring in the fourth stage. However, note also that there is no volva or cup—an earmark of Amanitas.

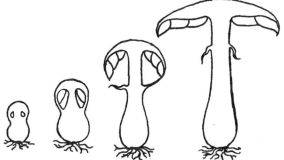

Growth of the Meadow Mushroom

A few of the more common species will be given here. They grow in sufficient numbers to readily fill the baskets of the epicures.

Common Meadow Mushroom
Agaricus campestris
Edible

Above:
Rodman's Mushroom
Agaricus rodmani
Edible

Below:
Fairy-Ring Mushroom
Marasmius oreades
Edible

USDA Photo

Fairy-Ring Mushroom
Marasmius oreades
Edible

COMMON MEADOW MUSHROOM
Agaricus campestris

Description: Because of its delicate pink gills in one stage, the Common Meadow Mushroom is sometimes called the "pink bottom." There are several varieties—most of them cultivated. Because these varieties are similar in shape and coloring, and all are edible, it is not necessary for the novice to trouble about details if he happens to find these plants growing in the fields, vegetable gardens, or pastures. Gather them and enjoy the feast.

The cap is at first hemispherical, then spreads with an incurved outer edge, or is nearly plane. The cap is cream-white, smooth, silky, or sometimes slightly hairy; the rim of the cap extends slightly beyond the gills. The flesh is rather thick, firm, and white. The gills are at first white, then a delicate pink, and in age a dark, almost black-brown; free from the stem and close together. The spores are purple-brown.

The stem is usually slightly thickened toward the base; white in color, stuffed on the inside and smooth, or nearly so, on the outside, with a ring near the middle which is usually more or less torn, and sometimes fallen away. The plant is from two to four inches high and from one and one half to four or five inches broad.

Where and When to Find It: The Common Meadow Mushroom is found throughout the United States, chiefly in fields, vegetable gardens, and pastures. You may find them on parking strips, in your lawn—or on the golf course; but you will not find them in the woods. They are most plentiful in late summer and fall.

Comment: *Edible.* This is one of the choice, edible mushrooms, and much has been written on ways to prepare them. However they are prepared, though, remember: these mushrooms should *never be peeled* before cooking, as peeling robs them of a great deal of their flavor.

There are several varieties of *campestris* and most of them are cultivated. In the United States, it is the only mushroom raised on a large scale for marketing. The bulk of this crop is grown near Philadelphia, where the industry began in 1904. Mushrooms also are raised in the vicinity of New York, Chicago, St. Louis, and large cities on the West Coast. The mushroom cellars where they are grown must be carefully controlled in temperature and humidity.

Excellent as many of the commercially grown mushrooms are, they often do not equal the wild Field Mushroom in flavor or texture.

RODMAN'S MUSHROOM
Agaricus rodmani

Description: Rodman's Mushroom is very much like the *campestris* except that its gills are smaller and its stem solid. The gills at first are white instead of light pink as in the Meadow Mushroom, but soon turn to a brownish-pink as the plant matures. The cap takes on a yellowish color as it matures. It grows to about three inches in height; and the cap from two to four inches across. The flesh is white and unchanged upon being cut or broken.

Where and When to Find It: Rodman's Mushroom makes its appearance on grassy ground about June, and can be found until late July. It grows especially large on rich soil in valley bottoms of the Northwest.

Comment: *Edible.* A tasty edible mushroom, but it lacks something of the delicate flavor of the Meadow Mushroom.

See color photograph 5.

COAST MUSHROOM
Agaricus maritimus

Description: This stubby, solid mushroom is well built to withstand the great winds and storms of its coastal home. Its cap is fleshy and firm; at first hemispherical, then broadly convex, and sometimes nearly flat, and occasionally with faintly marked scales. When young, the cap is white, changing to a dingy, grayish-brown in age. The flesh becomes reddish in color when cut, and gives off an odor of the sea. The gills are narrow, close-packed, and free from the stem; pinkish when young, becoming a purple-brown with age. The spore print is purple-brown.

The stem is about two inches long in the mature plant; it is firm, solid, and white, with a delicate ring that often disappears at early development.

Where and When to Find It: The hardy Coast Mushroom is common along both the Oregon and Washington coasts, as well as in pastures where the soil is sandy. It appears in greatest abundance during August and September; and if the weather has been warm, matures to a larger size than it does when the weather has been cold and foggy.

Comment: *Edible.* Growing near the sea, the Coast Mushroom seems to have taken on the odor as well as the slight tang of delicate seafood.

BELL MUSHROOM
Agaricus foederatus

Description: The Bell Mushroom is so-called because in maturity it swells out to a distinct bell-shape. Its cap is from two to three inches broad and fleshy; rather thin; at first ovoid, then swelling out to its bell-shape; then convex with a slightly depressed center and a slightly involute margin from which hang remnants of the veil. In color, the cap is tawny, and scaled with minute, white granules, somewhat scattered.

The four-inch stem is stout; hollow or stuffed with fibrous hairs; larger at the base. Below the ring it is rather rough. The gills are at first pinkish, growing to brown color with age. The spore print is brownish.

Where and When to Find It: The Bell Mushroom grows on the ground in pastures and meadows, and is found in summer, especially after warm rains.

Comment: *Edible.* Like the Common Meadow Mushroom, this is among the best of the Agarics.

RED-FLESHED AGARICUS
Agaricus elvensis

Description: The Red-Fleshed Agaricus is one of the most common of the Pacific Coast mushrooms, and is so-called because, when cut, the flesh turns red.

The cap is from four to six inches across; at first almost spherical, then hemispherical; covered with minute silk-like fibers, broken into large brown scales, which in turn are broken into little patches in the center. The margin is thick and covered with triangular-shaped warts.

The stem is from four to six inches high and about two inches thick in the center; hairy near the bottom; solid and stuffed with delicate fibers. The stem carries a thick, very large, deflexed ring that is broken here and there. The gills are crowded; free from the stem; of a brownish-flesh color. The spore print is brownish. The flesh, as mentioned, turns red when cut.

Where and When to Find It: The Red-Fleshed Agarics grow under trees. Although they are delicious, the casual hunter had better not indulge in the pleasure of gathering them unless he is very careful that they are isolated from the Amanita, always remembering that the Amanita has *white gills,* and the species here mentioned does not. Where oak trees are isolated, as they often are, especially in the southern part of Oregon, it is perfectly safe for the novice to gather the *elvensis.*

Comment: *Edible.* This mushroom is excellent either cooked or in salad.

CALIFORNIA AGARICUS
Agaricus californicus

Description: Like the Red-Fleshed Agaricus, the California species also grows under trees; but, unlike the Red-Fleshed, the meat of the California species—which is oyster-white—does not change color when bruised or cut. The cap is also covered with silky hairs, and is at first almost cone-like, becoming convex. The cap is whitish and tinged with purple or brownish-purple on the disk or center. The average breadth is three inches.

The gills are closely packed; free from the stem; at first pink, then becoming purplish, then almost black with a brownish tinge. The spore print is brownish-black. The stem is solid or stuffed, usually tapering upward to the ring where it narrows abruptly. In color the stem is usually of a brownish tinge, and about three inches in height in the matured plant.

Where and When to Find It: The California Agaricus can be found growing under isolated oak trees in Western Oregon and Washington—and in Northern and Central California (as its name suggests). It is most plentiful in the autumn months. In gathering the *californicus,* observe the same precautions as with *elvensis,* since both grow under trees.

Comment: *Edible.* Like a number of related species, the California Agaricus is a tasty mushroom.

HORSE MUSHROOM
Agaricus arvensis

Description: This big beauty grows from two to five inches high and its cap often reaches a growth of six inches across. The cap is at first round, then bell-shaped, then flat. It changes from a rather scaly or mealy texture to a smooth white or yellowish, and the flesh is white.

The gills grow free from the stem and are broader toward the stem than at the outer edge; at first of a whitish color, then pale pink, and when the plant is old, a blackish-brown. The Horse Mushroom can readily be distinguished from the Amanitas and the White Lepiotas by these dark-colored gills at maturity. The spore print is purple-brown. The stem is smooth, hollow or stuffed; it carries a ring that is thick and rather large.

Where and When to Find It: The Horse Mushroom belongs generally to cultivated ground. It can be found in newly slashed areas, in fields and old grassy areas, especially after a warm rain in summer and fall.

Comment: *Edible.* The Horse Mushroom is either a form of the Common Meadow Mushroom, or closely related to it. It is a delicious species, though a little coarser in texture than the *campestris.*

BULBOUS AGARICUS
Agaricus magnificus

Description: The Bulbous Agaricus closely resembles the Horse Mushroom in both size and appearance. It takes its name from its bulbous base, shown clearly in the above drawing. The cap is from two to six inches broad; fleshy; thick; convex; becoming nearly flat and depressed in the center. The cap is bare and often split and wavy on the margin. It is a white or whitish color; often tinged with brown in the center.

The gills are rather broad and free from the stem; bellied, white in color, becoming a purplish-brown with age, but never pink. The novice should gather this mushroom only when the gills have become dark. The spore print is dark. The stem is from four to six inches high; firm; stuffed with pith; bulbous or thick at base; ringed with the ring firmly attached. The stem is whitish in color.

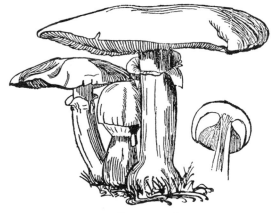

BULBOUS AGARICUS
Agaricus magnificus

Where and When to Find It: Like the Horse Mushroom, the Bulbous Agaricus can be found in the more cultivated lands and in newly slashed areas; occasionally in thin woodlands. It is a fall species.

Comment: *Edible.* The Bulbous Agaricus has a good flavor and is tender throughout when young, but as it gets old, the stems are inclined to be tough. The novice though, is advised to gather the mushroom only when the gills have become dark with age—to be safe from confusing it with the Amanitas or the White Lepiota. The caps are still excellent and he can discard the stems if he wishes.

FLAT-CAP MUSHROOM
Agaricus placomyces

Description: At maturity, the Flat-Cap is domed, later flattening out; hence its name. The cap is three to four inches across, and dark brown to gray scales appear as broken patches over the surface, except at the center where they form a solid covering. The gills vary in color from pink to gray-brown. The spore print is brownish. The partial veil becomes a pronounced ring on the stem as shown in the drawing above. The flesh often turns pink with age; the stems are three to four inches long at maturity.

Where and When to Find It: The Flat-Cap grows abundantly in Western Oregon and Washington in the moist, deciduous woodlands. It occurs most commonly from September through November.

Comment: *Edible* but not recommended because some persons have reported ill effects from it. Possibly its reputation suffers from the fact that variants of the species can cause mild poisoning. The Flat-Caps usually have a slight antiseptic odor.

FAIRY-RING MUSHROOM
Marasmius oreades

Description: The Fairy-Ring Mushroom, *Marasmius oreades,* so common in America and Europe, grows in circles, as the name implies. Some other species of mushrooms also grow in circles, but *oreades* is now generally the species referred to as the Fairy-Ring. It is included here with Agaricus because it also favors grassy areas and is likely to be encountered by the pot-hunter searching for Meadow Mushrooms. In folklore, such a ring was regarded as the dancing court of fairies, who visited blindness or sickness upon any mortal who trod upon it.

The rings can appear as circles of rank or withered grass (trodden down by the dancing fairies)—often seen in lawns, meadows, and grass plots. In sober truth, these rings are simply the mushroom or fungus below the surface, which has seeded circularly, as many plants do. When the ring is brown and almost bare, the "spawn" has enveloped the grass roots and thus prevented their absorbing moisture; but when the grass is luxuriant, the "spawn" itself has died, and served as manure to the young grass. The lovely white Fairy-Ring is part of this cycle of growth.

The caps of the Fairy-Rings—sometimes called Scotch Bonnets—are from one to two inches broad; reddish-brown in color; becoming pale when absorbing moisture, and whitish when dry. At first the cap is round, then it flattens out, with a slight knob in the center as illustrated. The cap is smooth and slightly irregular at the margin when moist.

The stem is two to three inches long; solid and very tough. Usually straight, it is nearly equal from top to bottom, and covered with a downy-woven cuticle that can be rubbed off. The stem is bluntly rooted and has no covering. The gills are free from the stem and alternating short and long. At first soft, they become firmer and are pallid-white in color. The spore print is white.

Where and When to Find It: The Fairy-Ring must be sought where the grass is luxuriant. It hides in it and is well worth the search. It favors open areas: lawns, golf courses, parking strips, and fields and meadows. It usually forms a full or partial circle. It is most plentiful from spring through fall, but in mild climates it may be found most of the year.

Comment: *Edible.* The Fairy-Ring Mushroom is good raw, cooked, or dried. When eaten raw, fresh or shriveled, it is sweet, nutty and succulent; stewed well, or cooked in almost any manner, it is delicious. Though slightly tough, its consistency is agreeable, and the most delicate stomachs can digest it. In Europe, it is given to patients recovering from operations or a dangerous illness, and at one time was given to patients in a large hospital in Philadelphia, where it was used with marked beneficial effects.

When dried by exposure to the air or sun, the Fairy-Ring Mushroom can be kept indefinitely, and does not lose its aroma or flavor, which are brought out in cooking.

See color photograph 6.

INKY CAPS (*Coprinus*)

Coprinus mushrooms are commonly called Inky Caps and are very plentiful in almost all localities. Everyone has seen one or more of the species growing on lawns, in fields or pastures by the roadside, or along streets. Some grow on manure piles or well-fertilized soil, and some grow on wood. The species are all of delicate body, and most of them disappear in a day.

The Coprinus, in its young growth, has gills free from each other, but closely packed; as the plants age and the spores ripen, the entire gill structure becomes black and dissolves into an inky fluid, the color of which is due to the spores; hence the name, Inky Caps.

The blackening of the gills in the Coprinus is not a process of decay, but is due to the growth of the spores; and the plant —before it drips away—is still edible, although not so pleasing to the eye. The Coprinus is easily recognized and cannot possibly be mistaken for an Amanita because of the color of the gills. When the plant is mature, it stains the fingers upon contact.

Most of the species are small, but grow in such abundance that the pot-hunter can gather a dish in a very few minutes. They are tender, of real mushroom flavor, and very delicate to the taste.

Pioneers used the Inky Caps in making their own writing fluid. They boiled the mature plants, strained the fluid, and added a bit of corrosive sublimate to keep it from molding. While the ink was often rather pale, it held its own with walnut juice, or ink made from iron nails.

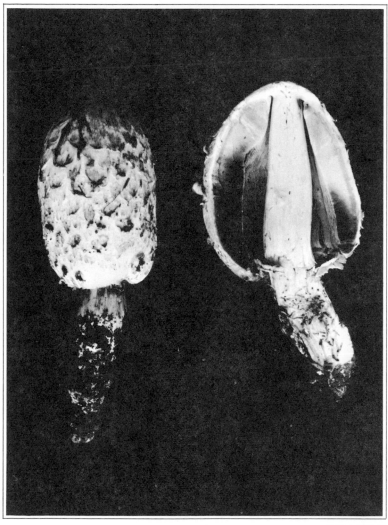

USDA Photo

Shaggy-Mane
Coprinus comatus
Edible

Shaggy-Mane in natural habitat

Mica-Cap Coprinus
Coprinus micaceus
Edible

USDA Photo

Inky Cap
Coprinus atramentarius
Edible

SHAGGY-MANE
Coprinus comatus

Description: The Shaggy-Mane is queen of the Inky Caps. It is from two to eight inches in height, and is one of the most beautiful and most edible of all fungi.

The cap is at first oblong, fleshy, and beautifully white; as it ages, it opens out and looks very much like a half-closed umbrella. When it reaches the mature and melting state, it splits at the margin along the line of the gills; the cuticle, except upon the apex, separating into shaggy scales—hence its name. These scales at times are yellowish or tinged with the inky-black shade of the gills.

The gills are free from the stem; crowded and at first tightly stuck together; broad; white; then tinged with pink or a faint salmon color; then purple to black as they drip away into ink. The stem grows up to ten inches long and is tapered upward, most of it being concealed within the cap; hollow, but with fine threads within; smooth or fibrillose; white or lilac-white; brittle, and easily pulled out of the cap. The ring around the stem is thin; torn—although sometimes whole; and it is movable.

Where and When to Find It: The Shaggy-Mane grows on rich lawns, in gardens, beside roads, and dumps, and where ashes have been placed. It grows either solitary or in large dense clusters, from mid-summer until early frost. When the spring rains are warm, the Shaggy-Mane pops up along roadsides and in lawns having a southern exposure, often two or three months before its usual appearance.

Comment: *Edible.* Very delicious in the young stage, but it should be eaten the day of harvest. The process of darkening works rapidly, and the Inky Cap soon dissolves into ink. Better not try to keep them in the refrigerator overnight—they will mature and the caps and gills will be dissolved by morning.

INKY EGG
Coprinus ovatus

Description: This is another Shaggy-Mane so similar to the *comatus* that it is often mistaken for it. The *ovatus* is called locally the Inky Egg. It is thinner, smaller, and not nearly so beautiful as the *comatus*, but grows under the same conditions, and is just as delicious when cooked.

The cap is white, and at first egg-shaped, and has the appearance of being thickly shingled over with thick, spreading, concentric scales; while the top is covered with an even hood, which expands and finally becomes striated—furrowed with radiating lines. The stem is from three to four inches long; solid at the base; otherwise hollow, with fine threads within, tapered upward; downy and shining white. The ring, not at any time very noticeable, soon disappears. The gills are free from the stem; remote—they do not extend the full distance from the margin of the cap to the stem; swelled out in the middle; at first free from spores and remaining shining white for a long time, then turning an umber-black—never becoming purple.

Where and When to Find It: The Inky Egg, like the Shaggy-Mane, grows on lawns, in gardens, and along roadsides, under very similar conditions to the Shaggy-Mane. They are often found together, and grow most profusely from midsummer until frost.

Comment: *Edible.* They are very delicious in the young stage, but must be eaten on the day of harvest. Unattractive as they are in the darker stages, they do not become poisonous.

INKY CAP
Coprinus atramentarius

Description: The name of this species—*atramentarius*—actually means black, or ink-like. This characteristic Inky Cap is from one to four inches across and oval-shaped. It is grayish, or grayish-brown; with occasionally a few hardly noticeable scales on the disk, and is often covered with a bloom—a delicate, powdery coating. The margin is ribbed, and often notched. The cap is tender and soft.

The stem averages five inches in length, and is about one-half inch thick; smooth; whitish; hollow; tapering upward, and has a more or less distinct ring near the base. The inside of the stem is obscurely banded, by which it may be recognized with certainty. The gills are free from the stem; bellied; crowded, and at first sticking together. The gills are white with edges spotted with small flecks; then becoming black and melting into ink. The spores are black.

Where and When to Find It: This Inky Cap grows singly or in clusters on rich ground, lawns, gardens, gutter-sides, or in the woods, but never on dung-heaps. It makes its appearance in the early summer and in the autumn. It is most abundant after rains and one crop succeeds another until frost. The Inky Cap is common in Europe as well as the United States.

Comment: *Edible.* The Inky Cap is of a stronger flavor than is the Shaggy-Mane, and should be cooked as soon as possible after gathering. Some persons have reported mild indigestion when combining this species with alcoholic drinks.

See color photograph 7.

LARGE-SPORED COPRINUS
Coprinus macrosporus

Description: This species of Inky Cap, the *macrosporus* (meaning "large-spored"), looks very much like some of the Lepiotas. It grows from one to two inches high. The cap is from one to two inches broad, although it sometimes grows larger, is oval, then expanded; cracks in lines around the edges; and is covered with tiny scales that overlap like tiles, or shingles. The color is white, although the small disk is brownish, and scaly.

The gills are free from the stem; crowded; white when young; growing black with age. The spores are black. The stem is white, with traces of a ring near the thickened base; smooth, and stuffed with fine hair-like fibers.

Where and When to Find It: The Large-Spored Coprinus grows in the open fields, most abundantly from July to September.

Comment: *Edible.* The flavor of this Coprinus is somewhat stronger than that of the other Inky Caps; like the others it should be used as soon as possible after being harvested.

DUNGHILL MUSHROOM
Coprinus fimetarius

Description: A distinctive feature of the Dunghill Mushroom is its root system. Sometimes the root is as long as the stem, which averages about three inches in length. The cap is from one to two inches across; at first shaped like a little cylinder, but soon becoming conical, the edge at length rolled downward and torn at the margin. When the plant is young, it is covered with tiny, tufted and projecting scales which are white; this is from the universal veil, which separates from the top toward the largest part, at length becoming naked. It is cracked lengthwise but does not open into furrows. The top, which remains entire, is discolored.

The stem is about three inches long; hollow; fragile; thickened at the base, tapering upward; shining white in color and downy with little scales of the same color. The gills are free from the stem (see sectional drawing below); at first swelling out in the middle, then straight; bent in a zigzag manner, becoming black with age. The spores are black.

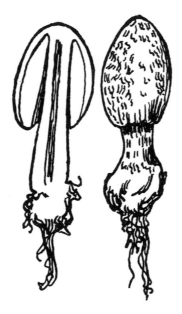

Dunghill Mushroom
Coprinus fimetarius

Where and When to Find It: This species takes its name from its habitat. *Fimetarius* comes from the Latin *fimus*, meaning dung or manure; and that is where you will usually find it, on manure heaps, where it thrives, much as do strawberries when exposed to similar treatment. The Dunghill Mushroom is common over the United States and in Europe, and it grows in successive crops from spring until the first frost.

Comment: *Edible.* The Dunghill has excellent flavor, is tender and plentiful. It should be cooked as soon as gathered—like the others of this genus.

VARIETIES OF DUNGHILL MUSHROOM

There are a number of varieties of the Dunghill species and all are edible and excellent. True to their genus name, *Coprinus,* several of them prefer the richness of the compost or manure heap. The word *Coprinus* itself comes from the Greek word for dung—*kopros.*

The following edible varieties occur in successive crops from spring until fall:

CLUSTER COPRINUS

This variety, the *Coprinus pullatus,* grows in clusters on manure heaps, with the cap at first covered with a loose, hairy veil, which soon becomes naked; brownish in color; then blackish. The stem is smooth.

ASH-COLORED COPRINUS

This variety, the *Coprinus cinereus,* is another very edible Dunghill Mushroom. It grows on manure heaps, as do the others. The cap is membranous, scaly, then naked. The stem is two to three inches long, hollow to the base; often twisted, and has no root.

LARGE-ROOT COPRINUS

This member of the Coprinus family (*Coprinus macrorhiza*) also receives its name from a distinguishing feature: *macro* (large), plus *rhiza* (*root*). This variety has an elongated rooting base, much like the *fimetarius.* The *macrorhiza* (the most common Dunghill variety) has a cap that at first is covered with feathery overlapping scales. It is a little paler and smaller than in typical form, with a stem shorter and an elongated rooting base. The stem is hairy and fragile.

The Large-Root Coprinus seems to take on different little habits. One form of it grows in the woods on rotted logs and stumps. Like other members of Coprinus it should be cooked as soon as gathered, as it is very fragile and soon grows beyond the cooking, or table-stage.

MICA-CAP COPRINUS
Coprinus micaceus

Description: The familiar Mica-Cap Mushroom, one of the most dependable, is easily distinguished by its lustrous top, which often shines like mica or isinglass.

The cap is from one to two inches in breadth; oval-shaped when it is young; growing to bell-shaped, with the margin more or less rolled back; wavy, splitting; closely lined with scattering scales and sparkling atoms, or sometimes naked; varying in color from whitish-yellow to livid-brown; darker when moist or old. The gills are narrow; crowded; white when young, then pinkish, growing black with age. The spores are black. The stem is slender, and about four inches in height in the matured plant; sometimes twisted; white in color; hollow; and of a silky texture and sheen.

Where and When to Find It: The Mica-Cap Coprinus makes its appearance in the early spring and has a continuous growth from month to month and year to year, clustered about trees, posts, along the grassy sides of pavements, in the fields, or at almost any place where there is sod. Only when the weather becomes very hot is there a letup in growth.

Comment: *Edible.* Although the Mica-Cap is small, it grows so plentifully that baskets are soon filled. It makes a rich and delicious dish, stewed in its own juices, or in milk. Feasts of it can be made until the frost checks its growth. As they quickly become "inky," cook them soon after gathering.

See color photograph 8.

GIANT PANAEOLUS
Panaeolus solidipes

Description: This handsome giant grows from five to a lofty eight inches in height. Though not a member of the Coprinus group, it is included in this section because the mushroom hunter will likely encounter it among the Coprinus plants and will wonder how it got there. The Giant Panaeolus also prefers the rich habitat of the dunghill. It is one of the most readily recognized species; of good weight and substance.

The cap is from two to three inches across; firm and at first hemispherical; then convex; whitish in color, the cuticle breaking up into rather large, angular scales that take on a dingy tinge. The scales are larger on the top than at the margin. The gills are broad, slightly attached to the stem; first white, then becoming black with age. The spores are black. The stem grows white, firm, and solid, slightly lined at the top; often it is found beaded with drops of moisture.

Where and When to Find It: The Giant Panaeolus grows on manure and compost heaps from early May until frost.

Comment: *Edible.* It makes an excellent dish, but because of its unsavory location, it, like the Coprinus, is sometimes bypassed by the hunter.

MILK MUSHROOMS *(Lactarius)*

The Milk Mushrooms, genus *Lactarius,* contain some fine edible species, but several with mildly poisonous characteristics. The finest of all is the *deliciosus,* and it can readily be identified by the novice. The Milk Mushrooms have no ring or cup; the gills are attached to the stem and often descend it a short distance. Most important: when the cap, gills, or stems are cut or broken, a milk-like or colored fluid (latex) is emitted.

DELICIOUS LACTARIUS
Lactarius deliciosus

Description: In cap, gills, stem, and latex or fluid, the Delicious Lactarius features orange. Sometimes it is even called Orange Delicious or Orange Delight. The cap is three to five inches in diameter at maturity, sticky when moist. It is convex when young, funnel-shaped when old. It is always some shade of orange color, from dark to pale, often with spots or zones of green. The cap does not easily separate from the stem.

The flesh is soft, spongy, brittle, white to orange. The gills are orange like the cap, narrow and close together, greenish when bruised or aged. The spore print is a pale pink. The stem is one to four inches long and one-half inch thick, frosted or covered with bloom at first, and orange like the cap, often with green streaks or spots. It becomes hollow with age. The milk— a bright red-orange fluid—seeps out when the cap, the gills, or the stem become cut or broken. There is more of this fluid in the young *deliciosus.* If this fluid is white, the novice is advised to discard the specimen.

Where and When to Find It: The Delicious Lactarius grows in coniferous woods, on the ground, generally in mossy areas along streams. It is most plentiful from July till November.

Comment: *Edible* and safe for the novice to gather, and highly prized as food.

See color photograph 9.

Delicious Lactarius
Lactarius deliciosus
Edible

WOOD-GROWING MUSHROOMS
(*Pleurotus, Armillaria*)

Mushrooms grow in a number of shapes and forms, and in a variety of places. On the Pacific Slope there are dozens of wood-growing mushrooms—sometimes called "shelf" or "bracket" mushrooms because of their shelf-like formation. When one of these mushrooms occurs in the wound of a tree, it will often spread under the bark and cause the death of the tree.

Included here are three of the wood-growing species which the pot-hunter will likely encounter in his search through the woodlands—the Oyster Mushroom, the Honey Mushroom, and the Velvet-Stemmed Collybia.

OYSTER MUSHROOM
Pleurotus ostreatus

Description: The popular wood-growing Oyster Mushroom and its many companions are common from our northern boundary to the gulf. Deer are quick to find this "shellfish of the forest" and claim the dainty morsels for their own. It is said that cows are attracted by its scent even if it is deep under snow. When a growth of the Oyster Mushroom is once found, plants can be kept growing for a whole season by watering the spot from which they were first taken.

Oyster Mushroom
Pleurotus ostreatus
Edible

USDA Photo

Velvet-Stemmed Collybia
Collybia velutipes
Edible

Honey Mushroom or Oak Fungus
Armillaria mellea
Edible

Honey Mushroom or Oak Fungus
Armillaria mellea
(Cluster)
Edible

The cap of the Oyster Mushroom is from two to five inches broad; when young it becomes almost black; soon growing pale, brownish-ash color; then passing into yellow when old. The cap is then fleshy, soft, shell-shaped, smooth, moist and even, but sometimes with the cuticle torn into scales. The cap may grow directly from the wood on which it is living, or it may have a short stem. In either case it is usually attached laterally rather than centrally to the wood. If the caps are growing directly from the top of the wood, they may be almost centrally attached. The stem, when present, thickens upward and is white. The gills are broad and white, sometimes turning a light yellow. They grow down onto the stem; long in front and short behind, where the cap grows down. The spores are lilac color. Actually, there are several varieties of Oyster Mushrooms, but all are edible.

Where and When to Find It: The Oyster Mushroom grows on all sorts of trees, fallen or standing, dead or alive. Wood is its favorite habitat, and it is plentiful from early spring till fall.

Comment: *Edible.* Dipped in egg, rolled in bread crumbs and fried, this is a vegetable oyster truly worthy of the most regal menu.

HONEY MUSHROOM
Armillaria mellea

Description: Of the dozens of tree-growing mushrooms found on the Pacific Slope, perhaps the Honey Mushroom is the most plentiful. It is the bane of the orchardist, as once it takes hold of a tree, that tree likely dies. The Honey Mushroom swarms up the trunk of trees as small decayed places appear, soon covering the whole tree.

The cap is adorned with minute tufts of brown or blackish hairs, although sometimes it is smooth and even (no depressions or elevations); or when old, slightly furrowed on the margin.

The gills are bluntly attached to the stem, or extend slightly downward on the stem. The gills are white or whitish, becoming darker with age, and sometimes variegated with reddish spots. The stem is ringed; at length brownish toward the base.

HONEY MUSHROOM
Armillaria mellea

Some shade of yellow is the prevailing color of the Honey Mushroom, but this will vary from very light to almost purplish-brown.

The stems can be straight and slender, swollen in the middle, bulbous toward the base, or distorted by pressure. The stem is as variable in color as is the cap. The outside is firm and fibrous, sometimes furrowed; inside it is soft or hollow. The cap is one to six inches across; the stem one to six inches long.

Where and When to Find It: The Honey Mushroom grows on nearly any tree or woody plant, and occurs throughout the United States in summer and fall.

Comment: *Edible.* Recommended for stews and omelets; also very good fried in margarine or butter. However, to the orchardist, it is a warning that his tree may die.

See color photograph 10.

Velvet-Stemmed Collybia
Collybia velutipes

Description: The Velvet-Stemmed Collybia is readily recognized by its velvety, tawny-brown stem, which is 1 to 4 inches long. The cap is 1 to 3 inches broad, thin, convex, then upturned, smooth, sticky, and yellowish to brown. The species grows in dense clusters which often crowd the caps into irregular shapes. The gills are broad, usually rather far apart, rounded near the stem, and white or yellowish.

Where and When to Find It: The Velvet-Stemmed Collybia can often be found the year around, though it flourishes chiefly in the fall, continuing into winter. It is another of the wood-growing mushrooms, appearing on ground that contains decaying wood, on stumps, or even from wounds on living trees.

Comment: *Edible.* This is a tender, pleasantly flavored species.

CHANTERELLES *(Cantharellus)*

All the Chanterelles are edible; many are delicious; and all species, except *Cantharellus crispa*, grow on the ground in both woods and open places.

The Chanterelles are distinguished by their thick-edged gills which generally form a network, or are forked. The gills extend down the stem, sometimes in folds or wrinkles, to form a vase-like or funnel-shaped mushroom. Because of their blunt gill edges, the Chanterelles are considered by many scientists not to be true gill fungi.

YELLOW CHANTERELLE
Cantharellus cibarius

Description: The Yellow Chanterelle is one of the most popular edible mushrooms of the Pacific Slope. It is shaped much like a goblet as its genus name suggests; *Cantharellus* is the Latin for "drinking vessel."

This Chanterelle also has a very pleasant aroma. Its fluted and ruffled cap is uniformly yellow to orange; one to four inches across, convex when young, then like a wavy-margined cup, more or less depressed in the center.

It has no ring on the stem and no cup at the base. The stem and cap run together and the gills run down from the cap to form folds on the stem. The gills are blunt like branched veins, not sharp edged like those of the Meadow Mushroom. The stem is one and one-half to three inches long, thick and solid and firm and smooth, tapering downward. The flesh is white; the gills a pale yellow; the spores, yellowish.

Where and When to Find It: The Yellow Chanterelle grows in coniferous woods, on the ground, singly or in small groups. It occurs most abundantly in July and August, but may be found until late fall.

Comment: *Edible.* For many centuries the Chanterelle has been considered a delicacy of the table, and it is gaining in popularity very rapidly in the United States. Some of the finest canned Chanterelles are imported from Switzerland.

See color photograph 11.

Yellow Chanterelle
Cantharellus cibarius
Edible

TRICHOLOMAS *(Tricholoma)*

These white-spored and thin-gilled Agarics vary greatly in color as well as edibility. There are many species, generally rather large, with fleshy caps and stems. The partial veil is never present except for slight remnants in some of the very young species. Of the species of Tricholoma known to be edible, the safest, best and most famous is the Masked Tricholoma or Blewits.

MASKED TRICHOLOMA OR BLEWITS
Tricholoma personatum

Description: The Masked Tricholoma, very close to the Meadow Mushroom in popularity, would be a good commercial species. The cap of this attractive mushroom varies from lilac to purple, but occasionally is pale gray or almost white, the center becoming brownish with age. Two to six inches across, it is thick and smooth; convex when young, flattening out with maturity.

Because of its often-colorful cap, the *personatum* is sometimes called Blewits Mushroom — from the French *bluet,* cornflower. However, its showy, masking color, generally pales with age.

The margin at first is downy, and turned inward. The flesh is lavender or whitish. The gills are attached to the stem, notched near the point of attachment. They are solid, white, or colored like the cap, and swollen or bulbous at the base. The gills are lavender; the spores, pinkish.

Where and When to Find It: The Masked Tricholoma grows in woods and open areas, especially where there is much leaf-mold or highly fertile soil. Usually it appears in groups; seldom singly. It flourishes from September until frost.

Comment: *Edible.* For many centuries it has enjoyed a reputation for being a choice species of mushroom.

See color photograph 12.

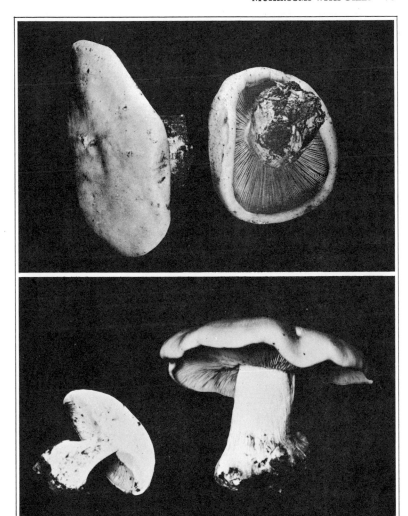

Masked Tricholoma or Blewits
Tricholoma personatum
Edible

USDA Photo

Equestrian Tricholoma
Tricholoma equestre
Edible

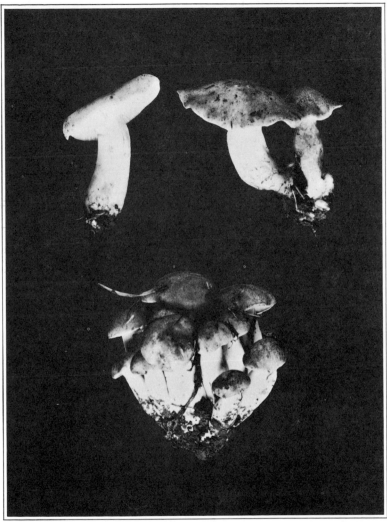

USDA Photo

Many-Headed Clitocybe
Clitocybe multiceps
Edible

CANARY TRICHOLOMA
Tricholoma equestre

Description: The cap of the Canary or Yellow Tricholoma is convex, becoming expanded. The margin of the cap is incurved at first, becoming slightly wavy and sticky. The color is pale yellow with brown or green overtones. The flesh is white or yellowish. The gills are a sulphur yellow, crowded, rounded and nearly free. The stem is stout, solid, and a light yellow. The cap reaches 2 to 3 inches across; the stem 1 to 2 inches in length, and one-half to three-fourths inch in thickness.

Where and When to Find It: The Canary Tricholoma grows on the ground in woods, especially pine woods, where it occasionally forms irregular fairy rings. It is a sturdy plant, often pushing its way out of the ground through a thick layer of pine needles. These needles sometimes cling so closely to the cap that the only indication of the presence of the mushroom is a small elevation. Its growth period is from fall till frost.

Comment: *Edible.* This species is delicious when fried or used in soups, the latter having a delicate turkey flavor.

MANY-HEADED CLITOCYBE
Clitocybe multiceps

Description: The Many-Headed Clitocybe bears a very close relationship to the Tricholomas, because of its often sinuate or wavy gills and indented margin of the cap. The cap is convex, fleshy, firm, and thin, except on the disk. In the young plants it is sometimes quite brown, but usually becomes whitish, grayish, or yellowish gray. The flesh is white; and the gills are also white, growing close together. The stem is equal or slightly thickened, solid or stuffed, and firm. The cap is from 1 to 3 inches across and the stem 2 to 4 inches long. However, the species varies greatly in size, shape, and texture.

Where and When to Find It: The Many-Headed Clitocybe flourishes in the spring and fall, and grows in dense clusters which are often concealed by grass or stubble.

Comment: *Edible,* but individual tastes differ greatly regarding this species. Many consider it one of the tastiest mushrooms; others dislike it heartily.

Part II—Mushrooms without Gills

PUFFBALLS (*Lycoperdon, Bovistella, Calvatia*)

A Puffball is a Puffball to the novice. Scientifically, a Puffball may belong to the *Lycoperdon,* the *Bovistella,* or to the *Calvatia* families, but it is a Puffball just the same and it is common in all parts of the world.

Puffballs are so-called because of their globular or pear-like shape, and their manner of discharging ripe spores in a smoke-like cloud when pressed or struck.

They have been called the "Stomach Fungi" because of their habit of producing spores inside the fruiting body. The spores are released through a small, circular opening at the top of the mushroom, or through a break in the wall. This family lacks true stems and caps, though some have a stem-like base.

As in members of the human race, different characteristics develop in different environments. In the mild climate of the Pacific Northwest, with plentiful rainfall and sunshine, fungi of many varieties flourish, sometimes almost beyond species recognition.

They are recommended for eating only in the young stages, when, on being cut clear through, they are white or whitish-colored. Do not eat those that have a touch of yellow. In the case of all the small Puffballs, a single one which has turned yellow, in the slightest degree, will spoil a whole dish.

When they are firm, before the flesh begins to soften, they are not only edible, but delicious. From those too minute to make it worth while for a hungry man to gather, to those so large that a single Puffball will furnish a meal for a whole family, they are edible when young and firm.

USDA Photo

Pear-Shaped Puffball
Lycoperdon pyriforme
Edible

Giant Puffball
Calvatia gigantea
Edible

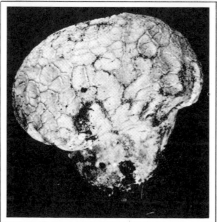

Skull Puffball
Calvatia craniformis
Edible

Pennsylvania State University

Puffballs, regardless of size or shape, if gathered fresh, are good in stews, gravies, sauces, or fried. Pickled in brine or vinegar, canned or dried, one can make no mistake, or go hungry, in a neighborhood where Puffballs abound. Used alone, or combined with raw vegetables, they make an excellent and delicate salad.

In the case of all Puffballs, gather and eat the young ones only; they should be firm and white clear through. As they mature the color and interior texture change and their use is not recommended. If they are small, cut through the center to be sure you have not gathered a white Amanita. The Puffball is solid white flesh; the Amanita shows the outline of a cap and stem.

LITTLE CHINK PUFFBALL
Lycoperdon rimulatum

Description: The Little Chink Puffball generally grows in groups. Although it is small—being only about an inch and a half in diameter and seldom over an inch in height—it is good eating. Its shape is broadly egg-shaped, with the broad end toward the apex. When young, the skin is thin and smooth, of a bluish-gray color. As it grows older, it breaks into a network of fine lines, which a little later turn into minute and thin scales, finally falling away from the smooth grayish or purplish surface of the inner peridium.

Where and When to Find It: The Little Chink is found in the woods, growing on the ground, and in the open fields. It is most abundant in the fall till frost.

Comment: *Edible.* Excellent when very young and tender. It darkens in the center when past the table stage of maturity.

LITTLE FOOT PUFFBALL
Lycoperdon pedicellatum

Description: This is one of the fuzzy-wuzzy Puffballs. It is an inch to an inch and a half in diameter; globe shaped, narrowing down into a stem-like base. It is a whitish, or light ash color, becoming brown with age; covered with spines which may be straight, slightly curved, or both. As the plant grows older, these spines fall off and leave slight impressions on the surface.

The Little Foot Puffball takes its name from the "little foot" or supporting stem.

Where and When to Find It: It grows in the woods, and in brush lots, on the ground; and on decaying wood and bark. It is most abundant in fall until frost.

Comment: *Edible,* yet it has less flavor than most of the Puff-balls. When the Little Foot passes the table-stage, it shows greenish-yellow, then dingy-olive in the center.

SMOOTH PUFFBALL
Lycoperdon glabellum

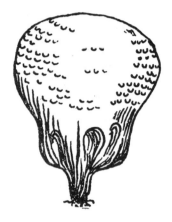

Description: Unlike many of the small fuzzy, or spine-covered, Puffballs, the Smooth Puffball is covered only with tiny, nearly uniform warts that, to the naked eye, are of a yellowish tinge. The outer covering or peridium is one to two inches in diameter, and often narrows down into a stem-like base. When the meat becomes purple-brown, it is not fit for table-use.

Where and When to Find It: The Smooth Puffball grows in the woods, after the first fall rains, and until the frost arrives.

Comment: *Edible.* When firm and solid, it makes a good dish; it is sweet tasting, delicate, and attractive.

EXCELLENT PUFFBALL
Lycoperdon eximium

Description: This is another of the small fuzzy-wuzzy mushrooms. It is nearly egg-shaped, with the wide end toward the top. The skin is white or tinged with brown, composed of long, slender spines, often curved and converging at the top. Later, these spines fall away from above, leaving a smooth surface. The Excellent fuzzy-wuzzy Puffball is about one and one-half inches in diameter, and one inch high.

Its species name, *eximium*, harks back to the time when there was a commonly used adjective, "eximious," meaning choice, select or excellent.

Where and When to Find It: The *Excellent* species grows on the ground in more or less sandy soil and is abundant in the fall.

Comment: *Edible.* As its name suggests, it is excellent eating—when young and tender.

CURTIS PUFFBALL
Lycoperdon curtisii

Description: Named for the man who is first known to have identified it, the Curtis Puffball is another of the fuzzy-wuzzy Puffballs, and it is just what you would expect a Puffball to be—round and fuzzy.

It has a very short-rooted base. The skin is a pale yellow, covered by a coat of soft, fragile white spines, curved and convergent at the top. After maturity the coat disappears, leaving a smooth surface. This little Puffball is only about an inch in diameter and grows in groups. It has many stems from the same root, often forming a thick carpet, or mat.

Where and When to Find It: The Curtis Puffball grows on the ground, in meadows, pastures, cultivated fields, and along the roadsides; from late summer till frost.

Comment: *Edible.* Like the other small Puffballs mentioned, it is a tasty dish when it is young and tender, and the flesh is firm.

GEMMED PUFFBALL
Lycoperdon gemmatum

Description: The Gemmed Puffball gets its name from the large erect spines or warts which stud its upper surface. This, the most common of the fuzzy-wuzzies, is known in all countries because it is found in almost every part of the world. It is about two inches in diameter and three inches high; more or less elongated and tapering; whitish or gray in color.

Where and When to Find It: The Gemmed Puffball grows on the ground and on logs in the woods from midsummer till late fall.

Comment: *Edible.* While it is equal in taste to any of the Puffballs, care must be taken in selecting the specimens before cooking. As with the other small mushrooms, a single one which has turned yellow in the slightest degree, will spoil a whole dish.

PEAR-SHAPED PUFFBALL
Lycoperdon pyriforme

Description: These little Putffballs were named for their shape —*pyrum* being the Latin for "pear." Like the Gemmed species, these are also known the world over. Of a dingy white in color, they are covered with tiny warts or scales, often with a few spines, resembling the fuzzy-wuzzies.

Where and When to Find It: The Pear-Shaped Puffball grows in clusters both in the woods and in cleared fields, on decaying wood and on the ground. It is found throughout the growing season, but is most plentiful in September and October. Often great masses of it will be found where a stump or log has rotted, leaving the ground covered with the decayed wood.

Comment: *Edible.* When raw, it smells and even tastes very much like the half-rotted wood of a fir. When cooked, if only the young and firm are used, they are fairly good. Remember: a yellow-tinged one can spoil a stew or make it rather bitter. For its reputation in the kitchen, we recommend the Gemmed Puffball over the Pear-Shaped species.

ONION PUFFBALL
Lycoperdon cepaesforme

Description: This little onion-shaped Puffball, the *cepaesforme* (Latin *cepa*—onion), is about one and one-half inches in diameter, white and smooth.

Where and When to Find It: It grows on the ground in fields and pastures and is most plentiful in September and October.

Comment: *Edible* and good.

CUP-SHAPED PUFFBALL
Calvatia cyathiformis

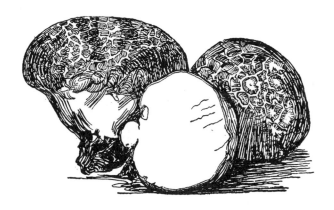

Description: The Cup-Shaped Puffball is common in all parts of the United States. It reaches from three to six inches in diameter, has a short, thick, stem-like base, and is a whitish-brown, or pinkish-brown on top. The top part of the Puffball, together with the outer covering or "bark," make up the peridium. The peridium of this species, *cyathiformis*, is shaped like a depressed globe. The surface is smooth—often with tiny scales, if the rain has not reached them nor the wind blown them off. The upper part often cracks into areas, as shown in the illustration.

The species was named for its cup-shaped base: Latin *cyathus* (cup) plus—*form* (form).

Where and When to Find It: The Cup-Shaped Puffball grows on open, grassy ground, usually from late June until frost.

Comment: *Edible.* It is usually plentiful, meaty, and of excellent flavor, but must be gathered before it turns dark. Not only people, but cows, deer, mice, squirrels, and the crickets are fond of the Cup-Shaped Puffball.

SKULL PUFFBALL
Calvatia craniformis

Description: The Skull or Cranium Puffball has a peridium measuring three to six inches in diameter and about five inches in height, unless the conditions under which it grows are very favorable; then it grows much larger. It is ovoid or egg-shaped; slightly depressed above, and has a thick base with a cord-like root. The skin is smooth, very thin, and easily peeled or wiped off. It is a very fragile fungus, of a grayish color, sometimes with a rusty tinge.

Where and When to Find It: The Skull Mushrooms grow on the ground in the woods, and are most generally found from August to November.

Comment: *Edible.* When young they are white and have a strong but pleasant odor, and are very good to eat. When they begin to change to yellow, they become bitter.

GIANT PUFFBALL
Calvatia gigantea

Description: The Giant Puffball is indeed a giant. In this country, it is sometimes three feet in diameter, but is said to be even larger in Europe. The average size here is ten to twenty inches in diameter. I have often found them so large that a single slice must be halved, in order to get it into an average-size frying pan. They have been reported up to forty-seven pounds.

GIANT PUFFBALL   *Calvatia gigantea*

The Giant Puffball has no stem or distinct base. It is attached to the earth by cord-like strands. It is usually round like a ball or egg-shaped, depressed in the center. The outer surface is smooth but often slightly rough, like chamois to the touch. Sometimes the surface is covered by minute warts; often it cracks in areas. It is white or whitish, changing to yellow or brown. The inner substance is pure white at first, changing to yellowish, and finally to dingy olive-brown with the ripened spores.

A spore print never needs to be made from Puffballs; the color of the spores is clearly seen when the inside of the ball becomes dry and powder-like.

Where and When to Find It: The Giant Puffball occurs singly or in groups of a few, on lawns, in pastures, meadows, and in open woods, usually in late summer or early fall.

Comment: *Edible.* The Giant Puffball is highly sought for food. If one is found in your neighborhood, it is often advisable to leave it where it grows, and slice from the top, as you need it. The cut surface dies, protecting the rest of it. The plant, after being cut, will not ripen further and fresh Puffball steaks may be cut for several days.

The larger specimens are excellent sliced and fried in a batter of eggs and bread crumbs. First, remove the thin outer rind. Puffballs are also good stewed, deviled, in soup, in salads, and prepared as croquettes.

When it passes the table-stage, the center becomes a yellowish-green and then a dingy-olive color, and a slight moisture forms in the center.

In its dry stage, the Giant has been used as a tinder, as a sponge and as a styptic in hemorrhage. The peasants of Northern Europe make a remedy of it for diarrhea in calves, and burn it under bee-hives, to stupefy the bees in order to rob them of their honey.   *See* color photograph 13.

Etched Puffball
Calvatia caelate

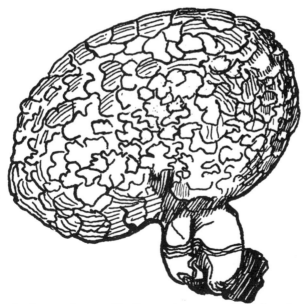

Description: This Puffball is often mistaken for the Giant, as it grows very large, but it is easily distinguished by its stem-like base. The Etched Puffball grows from four to ten inches in diameter, narrowed below into a short, thick, stem-like base. It is white in color, and the top breaks up into scales or warts, which later disappear.

Its species name, *caelate*, or "Etched," goes back historically to Roman times and the Latin engraving tool, *caelum*.

Where and When to Find It: The Etched Puffball grows in meadows, fields, and in old pasture land; also along roadsides. It is most common in the late summer and early fall.

Comment: *Edible.* Like its sister species, the Giant Puffball, it is excellent when young and may be prepared in a variety of ways.

BROAD-BASED PUFFBALL
Bovistella ohiensis

Description: This little Puffball belongs to the genus Bovistella rather than to the Lycoperdon or Calvatia genera. Its peridium measures from one to one and one-half inches across. It is nearly ball-shaped, with a thick, cord-like stem, as seen in the drawing above. Dirty-white when young, it becomes buff-colored in maturity.

Where and When to Find It: The *ohiensis* grows in open woods, in fields, and in old pastures, on the ground, and is most abundant in late fall.

Comment: *Edible.* Like the other Puffballs, it must be young to be tender and sweet.

You have now been introduced to a few of the sisters, cousins, and aunts of the Puffball family. There are a dozen others, all living within the law, and all bearing such a strong family resemblance that you cannot mistake them.

Note the Puffball family characteristics in the following related species: no cap or regular stem, and the base attached in the soil to the threads of the mycelium—the underground part of the mushroom plant. There is one important feature, though, that they do not have in common: size. They range from the tiny Puffball with a peridium of one-half inch to giants measuring several feet across.

Dwarf Puffball
Lycoperdon pusillum

Colored Puffball
Lycoperdon coloratum

Pointed Puffball
Lycoperdon acuminatum

Turner's Puffball
Lycoperdon turneri

SPONGE MUSHROOMS, the True Morels
(*Morchella*)

The Morels, sometimes called sponge mushrooms, are considered by epicures as superior in flavor to most of the mushrooms. They are easily identified by their thick stem and large, fleshy, sponge-like cap or head. They have neither gills nor tubes under the cap; nor does the stem have a ring or cup. The spores are produced on the outer surface of the cap in tiny sacs called *asci*. The pits in the cap which carry the spores may be short or long, deep or shallow, according to the species.

Known as the true Morels, the *Morchella* genus belongs to the large Helvellaceae family, most of whose members grow in the Pacific Northwest. All of them seem to grow larger and of a deeper color in the states of Oregon and Washington than they do elsewhere, unless it is in the northern part of California. They are generally edible, with an agreeable odor.

There has never been a suspicion cast on any of the Morels. They are eaten the world over, wherever found. European peasants formerly burned forests, so it is said, to insure a bountiful crop. It is one of the few species known to our pioneer fathers, and present-day farmers.

The Morel is usually found growing in ground that has been burned over, but this is not always true. It loves old apple orchards, especially those planted by pioneers, who used ashes around their trees. The Morel is often found in thinly wooded tracts, and growing along the edges of woods. The Morel dries well and keeps well for winter use.

The most common Morel found on the Pacific Slope is the Cone-Shaped species.

Pennsylvania State University

Species of Sponge Mushrooms or True Morels
Morchella

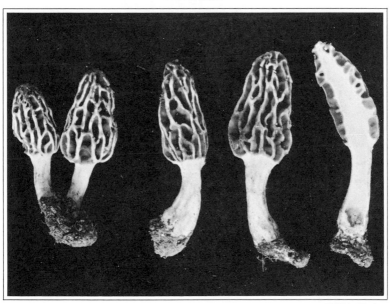

USDA Photo

Sponge Mushroom
Morchella esculenta
Edible

CONE-SHAPED MOREL
Morchella conica

Description: The Cone-Shaped Morel has a conical cap, or oblong-conical, as its name indicates. The longitudinal ridges on its surface run more regularly from top to base than in the *esculenta*. The color of the young plant is somewhat buff, becoming darker as it grows older. The matured plant as it grows in the Cascades and Coast ranges is often a pale slate color.

The stem, both delicate and brittle, is two to three inches long, and about one inch in diameter. It is hollow.

Where and When to Find It: It likes the thinly wooded areas, especially old apple orchards; the edges of woods or creek banks; and burned-over land. It grows on the ground, and a wet season is best for its development.

Comment: *Edible.* The Cone Morel is a highly prized species. It dries well and can be kept for winter use this way because flavor is maintained. In preparation for cooking, it is advisable to soak Morels overnight in salt water to remove insects or insect larvae hiding in the pits or ridges.

SPONGE MUSHROOM
Morchella esculenta

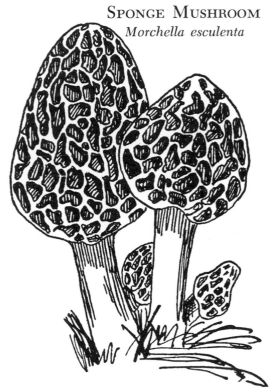

Description: This Sponge Morel is the best known in the genus *Morchella,* and one of the most edible. Its species name *esculenta* is mindful of our adjective "esculent," meaning edible. Also, this Morel is easily identified by its pits, which are more distinct than others of this group; and by its more obvious sponge-like shape.

It appears that the western variety of this species has pits a trifle longer than does the eastern variety, although not so long and narrow as those of the Cone-Shaped Morel. Some authorities contend that these are one and the same species. However that may be, both species, or rather, Morels with these separate characteristics, are to be found on the Pacific Slope.

The *esculenta* is variable in form, size, and color. It is usually broader than it is long. It is oval, at times tapering to a rounded top. The cavities, or pits, resemble those of a weather-beaten honeycomb, and are whitish-ash, or brownish in color. It is about as broad as it is tall, being from one to three inches each way. The stem is stout, light-colored, almost even, and is either hollow or slightly stuffed.

Where and When to Find It: The Sponge Mushroom grows on the ground in deciduous woods and in burned-over woodlands and forests; it especially favors old orchards and is most plentiful in spring and early summer, but at high elevations may be found nearly all summer.

Comment: *Edible.* This is one of the best mushrooms. As with other species, it is advisable to soak specimens overnight, or parboil, to remove any lurking insects or larvae from the pits or ridges.

HALF-FREE MOREL
Morchella semilibera

Description: Note that, as shown in the above drawing, the margin of the *semilibera* is free from the stem. As the plant ages, the cap may split at the apex and become free from the stem for part of its length. The cap is one-half to two inches in diameter and one-half to one and one-half inches long. It is not much larger than the stem itself and gives the appearance of being merely an extension of the stem. It is dark yellowish-brown.

The stem is three to six inches high and one to one and one-half inches in diameter at the base. It is usually smaller beyond the base.

Where and When to Find It: The Half-Free Morel grows quite commonly through the deciduous woods of the Northwest, and is most plentiful in April and May.

Comment: *Edible.* It is very good when young and not strong flavored when aged. Like the other Morels, it is considered safe for beginners to sample. However, the beginner should always sample a small portion of what he considers an edible specimen, to find if he is allergic to it. Later is the time for the bounteous serving.

See color photograph 14.

FALSE MORELS *(Helvella, Gyromitra)*

Besides the *Morchella*, the large Helvellaceae family includes a number of other groups or genera. Some of these so closely resemble the True Morels that they are popularly referred to as the False Morels. Of these "False Morels," *Helvellae* or the Helvells are most widely known. Like the whole family of Helvellaceae, the Helvells are sac fungi — so-called because their spores are formed in a sac—in contrast to the mushrooms with gills, pores, and spines; and the coral mushrooms, all of which have naked spores.

The False Morels can usually be distinguished from the True Morels by a wrinkled or folded—rather than a pitted or deeply ridged—cap. More important for the beginner is the fact that he should be somewhat cautious in collecting them. Some of the so-called edible species have proved poisonous to various individuals.

The largest of the edible *Helvella* group is *Helvella californica*.

CALIFORNIA HELVELLA
(Helvella californica)

Description: The California Helvella is two to six inches in diameter, and grows from two to six inches in height. The top hangs loosely, almost carelessly, over the stem, more like a brown rubber hood that has been wrinkled somewhat by the

Above: *Below:*

California Helvella   **Slate Helvella**
Helvella californica   *Helvella lacunosa*
Edible   Edible

Above:

False Morel
Helvella infula
Poisonous

Below:

Slippery Leotia
Leotia lubrica
Edible

heat. It is rounded, arranged in folds, and occasionally saddle-shaped. It is veined and white underneath. Its color ranges from tan to velvety brown, the light often bringing out a purple sheen against a brown background. The stem is ribbed, forming pits running up and down.

Where and When to Find It: *Californica* is common in our woodlands and forests; along the Salmon River, and, in fact, almost anywhere in the Mount Hood district, as well as around Mount Jefferson.

It grows on the ground, usually near boulders. It seems to be more frequently found in old stream channels, where rocks have been left with crevices filled with the leaf-mold and dead fern of ages. I have also found them growing in places where fire has swept through the forest.

Helvella Californica can be found in abundance from June until frost.

Comment: *Edible.* This species is tender and juicy, tasting much better than it looks, but the beginner should be cautious in using all of the False Morels.

See color photograph 15.

Slate Helvella
(Helvella lacunosa)

Description: The Northwest variety of *lacunosa* very much resembles the *californica* in all save color. The *lacunosa* shades into slate color or brownish-black. It also has a wrinkled, folded top. The Latin *lacunosus* means "full of holes or hollows."

The slate-colored cap is two to six inches in diameter; the stem, a dusky color, sometimes shading into a dark slate color; hollow and ribbed on the outside, forming intervening cavities.

Where and When to Find It: The Slate Helvella grows in woodlands and forests, especially the Cascade Mountains of Oregon and Washington; on the ground, near boulders. It is abundant from June until frost; often growing alongside, or near, the *californica*.

Comment: *Edible.* It is tender and juicy, tasting very much like the *californica*.

See color photograph 16.

SLIPPERY LEOTIA
Leotia lubrica

Description: This member of the Helvellaceae family grows on the ground in the woods, usually under the same or similar conditions as do the *californica* and *lacunosa*. The cap is shaped like an irregular half-sphere; inflated; wavy; and the margin is blunt. The whole plant is a dull olive yellow. The stem is about two inches high, nearly equal—or more or less inflated—at the base; pulpy within at first, but growing hollow. The outside of the yellowish stem is covered with minute white granules.

These small, slimy mushrooms are without gills, pores, or spines, producing their spores in tiny sacs or *asci*. However, because of their caps and stems, at a distance they appear like gilled mushrooms.

Where and When to Find It: The Slippery Leotia grows gregariously or in small clusters on the ground in the woods; often near boulders in highly organic soil. It is plentiful in spring and early summer.

Comment: *Edible.* Slippery Leotia is good eating, and, although it is a small plant, usually enough can be gathered to make a bountiful meal.

See color photograph 17.

CURLED HELVELLA
Helvella crispa

Description: The *crispa* (curled) Helvella has a white cap two inches in diameter. It is wavy-margined, somewhat resembling a small saddle. The white stem has elongated grooves and is twisted.

Where and When to Find It: It grows singly or in small clusters in the woods or boggy areas throughout the Northwest. It is most plentiful in early spring.

Comment: *Edible.* The Curled Helvella is good eating, but the novice is urged to take regular precautions when sampling the *crispa.*

BRAIN MUSHROOM
Gyromitra esculenta

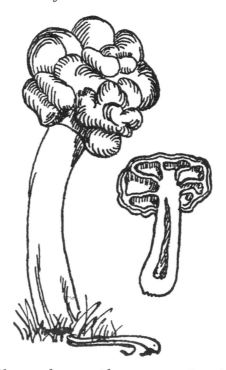

Description: Shown above, with a cross-section, is the Brain Mushroom, one of the long-known groups of Helvellaceae, with their characteristic convolutions and wrinkles. The cap is a reddish-brown and rounded, with many folds, much like a brain mass. The margin of the cap is attached to the stem in two or three places. When cut through, it is seen to be hollow, whitish and uneven within, with a few prominent irregular ribs or ridges. In large specimens, which may be four to five inches in diameter, it often appears as if two or more smaller ones were joined. The stem is stout, stuffed, or hollow; whitish and often irregular; and sometimes branched at the top.

Where and When to Find It: The Brain Mushroom is usually found in low wet places in evergreen forests, sometimes in the open, during the spring and summer.

Comment: *Poisonous.* Severe cases of poisoning have been reported from the Brain Mushroom, and scientists will tell you it is not edible, that it is even deadly. Nevertheless, this species presents one of the fine points in gathering mushrooms and eating them, wherein a practical person can find himself in conflict with authorities. I have eaten the species for thirty years and have found it very palatable; others have had similar experience.

The species name itself indicates that it used to be accepted as edible. *Esculenta* is from the Latin *esculentus,* meaning edible. Though now rare, there was a time when the English form, "esculent," was often used in general speech.

Nevertheless the Brain Mushroom, though long esteemed in Europe and parts of America, is now under strong suspicion, and the novice especially is warned to leave it strictly alone.

FALSE MOREL
Helvella infula

Description: The cap of this typical False Morel is two to three inches broad, smoother than most Helvellas, irregularly rounded, and often distinctly in the shape of a saddle. It ranges from light brown to a bay-red to brown. The stem is whitish and two to three inches long; thick, stuffed, or hollow.

Where and When to Find It: This saddle-shaped Helvella is commonly found in wet places or around springs, in sandy soils, and in decayed logs from conifer or deciduous trees. It occurs throughout the United States but is not prolific.

Comment: *Poisonous.* This species should definitely be regarded as dangerous as it has caused many cases of severe poisoning. It should never even be tasted, especially raw.

See color photograph 2.

BROWN GYROMITRA
Gyromitra brunnea

Description: The Brown Gyromitra, sometimes called Elephant Ears, is a stout, fleshy plant, three to seven inches high, with a broad, much contorted brown top. The stem is a little over an inch thick, more or less enlarged and spongy, and solid at the base.

Where and When to Find It: The Brown Gyromitra grows on the ground in rich soil or heavy leaf-mold of mixed woodlands. Usually several are found growing close together. It is most abundant from April till June.

Comment: *Edible.* The Brown Gyromitra is tender and possesses a fine flavor. Often the plants will weigh half a pound.

Egg-Yolk Mushroom
Mitrula vitellina

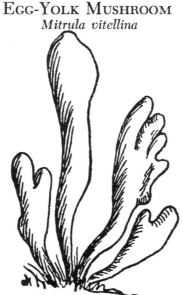

Description: This member of the large Helvellaceae group has caps, or clubs, curved and twisted in such a way that it is difficult to find two plants just alike. These plants, though, have an average height of only one or two inches, so they would scarcely be thought of as an important edible species—for a family anyway. Yet their beautiful bright yellow color makes them an attractive variety; in fact, they take their species name, *vitellina*, from the Latin *vitellus*, the yolk of an egg.

The irregular, lobed plant tapers from below into the short, distinct yellow club. Occasionally the club is more white than yellow.

Where and When to Find It: It grows in considerable profusion in wet mossy places in the woods, so, small as it is, a pint could soon be gathered. It is a fall species.

Comment: *Edible* and excellent. When one has found this species he will hunt for it again. Even when raw, cut in strips, it makes a delicious salad. Its flesh is tender and agreeable.

CORAL and CLUB MUSHROOMS *(Clavaria)*

Coral Mushrooms, *Clavaria,* are another group of fungi generally considered safe for the novice to gather. They vary in shape from the Little War Clubs (Latin *clava*—club) to the elaborate branching of the Crested Corals, and they bear their spores all over their outer surfaces.

The Corals grow in our forests and along the roadsides, from the Atlantic to the Pacific. Like the coral of the oceans, they come in delicate colors and pleasing shapes—white, orange, red, pink, delicate yellow and lavender. Their coloring and branching make them easy to distinguish.

Most of them are delicious either stewed or fried. I prefer them fried. Because of their brittleness they are often used in soups or gravies.

A few species are tough, and a few bitter, but the genus is plentiful and reliable. Many individuals are of marked excellence. Plants for the table should be young and fresh. When aged, or wormy, they should not be used. If stewed, they should be cooked slowly for about thirty minutes, and when fried, cooked slowly, and in an uncovered pan. They are crisp and delicious.

Often those growing among grasses, harmonize with the faded stalks under debris or the bleached surfaces of blades.

Those of the woods take the color of the leafmat or of the lichens, and the shapes of club and deerhorn moss, or grow in groves like little trees, with sturdy stems and twisted branches.

110

In the Crater Lake district of southern Oregon, the Corals, or *Clavaria*, push up their sturdy branches under the carpet of volcanic ash and pine needles, lifting the mass until cracks appear in the surrounding mat of needles. Often the Coral is twisted, flattened, and dwarfed in the struggle to break through. Deer, bear, and squirrels claw or paw the mats loose in order to reach the delectable food beneath, not waiting for the Corals to appear above the surface before they feast. Often during the long struggle in breaking through the mat of needles and ash, the plants become wormy and unfit for food.

The Corals grow in Oregon, Washington and California from sea level to timberline. I have found fresh specimens in the California redwoods and around Coos Bay, Oregon, in February. They can be found nearly the year around.

YELLOW CORAL
Clavaria fastigiata

Description: This is tufted, yellow Coral. It grows to about two inches in height; has numerous branches, flexible, or tough. The branches are more intricate when the plant grows under favorable conditions than when it grows under more restricted conditions, as when "grass bound," or forcing itself through dead grass stalks.

This species of Coral is commonly eaten in Europe. In Germany, it is called "goat's beard." As this type of Coral grows among tufted grasses, it must be looked for a little more closely than others.

Where and When to Find It: Yellow Coral is common. It grows in grassy glades, fields, and pastures during warm summer months.

Comment: *Edible,* and it has a very good flavor.

Amethyst Coral
Clavaria amethystina

Description: The Amethyst Coral grows from one to four inches in height; and, as its name implies, is of a violet or amethyst color. It is often very simple in structure, or very much branched. The branches are round, fragile, smooth, and even.

Where and When to Find It: This dainty bit of Coral graces the woods and grassy places, and is most abundant during warm spring and summer months.

Comment: *Edible* and excellent. It is a favorite in Europe and is eaten with great relish.

White Coral
Clavaria coralloides

Description: The White Coral grows to a height of from two to four inches. Under very favorable conditions, it often reaches six to eight inches. It is usually tufted, the tufts growing into each other. The trunk is thick, short, and much branched. The branches are repeatedly forked, compressed, hollow within, and fragile. Occasionally the branches do not develop entirely and are quite blunt.

Where and When to Find It: The White Coral grows in nearly every part of the United States during the summer months.

Comment: *Edible.* This is a common edible species in Europe as well as the United States. It is not always tender, but can always be used for flavoring purposes. When it is young and fresh, not only the branches can be eaten, but the upper part of the base.

Gray Coral
Clavaria cinerea

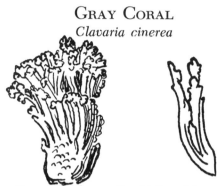

Description: Its gray color easily distinguishes this species from others, though it is variable in its mode of growth and in its shape. The Gray Coral grows from one to four inches in height. Sometimes it grows in clusters, either with a common base or separate bases. Occasionally it grows in rows. The stem is either thin or thick; short, and of a lighter color than the branches, which are numerous. The stem is wrinkled and irregular, somewhat blunt or flattened, and divided into slender points.

Where and When to Find It: This little Gray Coral grows in mixed woods, from the beginning of warm weather until frost, and is common throughout the United States.

Comment: *Edible.* It is a good table variety, but tough when old. Some claim the Gray Coral is injurious if eaten in quantities; others that it is edible, but provokes indigestion in delicate stomachs. I eat it and consider it one of the finest Corals that grows.

ROUND CORAL
Clavaria circinans

Description: Unlike the Amethyst, the Gray, and the Yellow Corals, this stumpy little fungus takes its name from its shape not its color; it grows in imperfect little circles in the woods. Its texture is solid and it is a dingy white color. It is one to two inches high, the branches being nearly parallel and of almost equal length.

Where and When to Find It: The Round Coral grows in the woods during summer and early fall.

Comment: *Edible.* While it is too tough to make an enjoyable meal, it is most excellent for flavoring.

GOLDEN CORAL
Clavaria aurea

Description: The Golden Coral grows from three to six inches in height. The trunk is thick, elastic, and pale. The flesh is white. This Coral divides into numerous thick branches that become repeatedly divided upward into two equal branches, terminating in slender, erect, round yellow branchlets. The color is not always a bright yellow, as its name, Golden, implies. Rather it is often a dingy-yellow, except where the sun and shade are nicely harmonized, and there is an ideal condition of moisture.

Where and When to Find It: The Golden Coral comes to the woods in the late summer.

Comment: *Edible.* This mushroom is tender and easily cooked.

CRESTED CORAL
Clavaria cristata

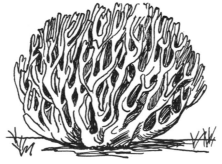

Description: The height of the Crested Coral is from one to five inches. Its whitish tufts of numerous broad, flattened branches grow from a short base. The many irregular branches are flattened upward and divided like moose horns. They are stuffed, and dingy in color.

The name Crested Coral comes from the tufted crown-like crest of the species.

Where and When to Find It: It appears after a warm summer rain, in rich wood-soil, where leaves and mold accumulate.

Comment: *Edible.* The Crested Coral is not as tender as some of the others, but cooked slowly, it makes a very enjoyable dish.

SPINDLE CORAL
Clavaria fusiformis

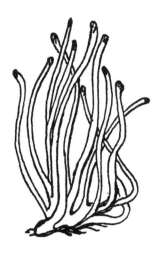

Description: The *fusiformis* (spindle-shaped) Coral is yellow in color, slightly firm, and grows hollow as it grows older. The clubs are about one-sixteenth of an inch through, and four inches or more in height. The light, clear yellow spindles are translucent, and clustered in groups of four or five that are united at the base.

Where and When to Find It: The Spindle Coral grows in woods and pastures, during warm weather.

Comment: *Edible.* This Coral is tender and well flavored but fragile.

YELLOW-TIPPED CORAL
Clavaria formosa

Description: This pale pink Coral grows from two to four inches in height. Its base is about one inch or more in diameter; whitish or yellowish. Its many branches are crowded, elongated, and divided at the ends into yellow branchlets which are thin, straight, and either blunt or toothed.

Where and When to Find It: The beautiful Yellow-Tipped *formosa* (from Latin *formosus,* beautiful) grows in deciduous or mixed woods in large tufts or rows several feet long. It is plentiful in late summer and fall.

Comment: *Edible but not recommended* as there have been, in recent years, many reports of unpleasant effects from it. It is a good idea to be cautious in eating any of the Corals with cream or pinkish flesh. If the flesh is at all gelatinous, the Coral should be discarded. The Gelatinous Coral *(Clavaria gelatinosa)* is generally regarded as poisonous; and, like the *formosa,* it often has yellow branch ends.

LITTLE WAR CLUBS
Clavaria pistillaris

Description: Some Little War Clubs are yellow; some almost orange and a little dingy. Others are a rich chocolate or a slate color. They grow from two to ten inches in height, and average one inch in thickness. The exterior is generally more or less wrinkled, usually with a smooth base. The meat is white, spongy, and fresh looking. The top of the club is puckered, as though it had been drawn in with a "puckering-string."

Where and When to Find It: From late June until after frost, one can find Little War Clubs in the woods of the Northwest. They often occur in clusters, growing in mixed woods from leaf-mold.

Comment: *Edible.* The more or less bitter taste in some specimens, when in the raw state, disappears when the mushroom is cooked. The Little Clubs are delicious.

CAULIFLOWER MUSHROOM
Sparassis radicata

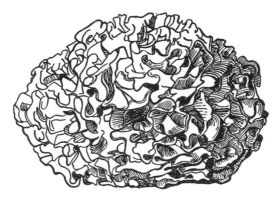

Description: The genus *Sparassis* of the club family of fungi (Clavariaceae) has long been identified with the Corals, though it differs technically. Its branches are flatter, more leaflike. Because of its similar character and appearance, though, it is being included here.

The large Cauliflower Mushroom is a beautiful and striking-looking plant—fleshy with flat leafy branches of a lettuce-like appearance. Its height is three to twelve inches; its width, four to twenty-four inches. It is whitish, buff, or pale yellow, and like a huge rosette, round and much folded. The folds are wide, with the flat branches rising from a common base. The surface of the leaves is dull.

Where and When to Find It: The Cauliflower Mushroom seems to be more common in the woodlands of Oregon and Washington than in any other part of the United States. It grows on the ground from spring till fall, but is not an abundant species. It is likely to be found in the Olympic and Rainier national forest areas, especially in the fall. Recently a fine specimen was discovered in the Mt. Hood area.

Comment: *Edible. Sparassis radicata* is delicious and keeps well. It can be easily dried, though shrinks considerably in the process.

PORE MUSHROOMS *(Boletes, Polypores)*

In Pore Mushrooms, examination of the under surface of the cap shows, not gills, but many small holes or pores. These holes are the ends of vertical tubes, side by side, and are called the tube mouths or pores. The spores are produced in the tubes, and spore prints can be obtained the same way as with the Gill Mushrooms. Some species of Pore Mushrooms have a ring, but they never have the cup or volva of the Amanitas.

Two large families of Pore Mushrooms are the Polypores ("many pores") or True Pore Mushrooms, and the Boletes or Fleshy Pore Mushrooms. Among the finest edible mushrooms are the large, fleshy Boletes, though they are unfortunately subject to early decay. The Northwest is fairly weighted down with thousands of pounds of these wholesome Bolete mushrooms from early summer until late in the autumn. Species of this genus are found from sea level to timberline. Some are as filling as a beefsteak, and taste very much like it. Others cook like pork, and are not unlike pork in flavor—pork with a mushroom-flavored sauce. Still others are of a lighter texture and more delicately flavored. Boletes are delicious in summer and autumn, fresh from the woods; or in winter—from your dried or canned supply—stewed, fried, broiled, or in gravies and sauces.

Boletes have both cap and stem and resemble the Gill Mushrooms in shape. Their flesh may change color when cut or bruised, but it never releases any milky fluid. Most species of Boletes are noted for the ease with which the tubes can be separated from the cap and from each other.

The few poisonous mushrooms in this genus are readily recognized by having more or less bright-red, orange-red, or dark-red coloring of the tube mouths. The novice should avoid this group and also those with dry caps that turn blue when they become bruised.

King Bolete
Boletus edulis
Edible

Rough-Stem Bolete
Boletus scaber
Edible

Two-Colored Bolete
Boletus bicolor
Edible

USDA Photo

Bitter Bolete
Boletus felleus
Edible

Pennsylvania State University

Hen-of-the-Woods
Polyporus frondosus
Edible

Sulphur Polypore
Polyporus sulphureus
Edible

Pennsylvania State University

While the writer eats most of the *Boleti,* the novice is cautioned against eating those likely to cause illness. One species in particular should be mentioned, the *eastwoodiae.* However, it has the distinctive tell-tale earmarks of the poisonous varieties: bright-red tube mouths, and the flesh of the cap becomes blue when broken or bruised. But there are plenty of Boletes in the Northwest with neither of these traits, so the casual pot-hunter need not go without these mushrooms on his dinner table.

ROUGH-STEM BOLETE
Boletus scaber

Description: The cap of the Rough-Stem Bolete is two to five inches across, convex to flat; usually smooth, but it may be pitted or wrinkled. The color varies from straw when young to dark brown when old or bruised. The tubes are whitish when the plant is young, but they darken as the cap does, with age. The stems are three to six inches long, solid, and roughened by dark dots or ridges.

Where and When to Find It: The Rough-Stem Bolete is confined largely to wet or open places in the woods. Sometimes it grows in open places in bushy areas. It is most plentiful during late July and August.

Comment: *Edible* and good.

STICKY-CAP BOLETE
Boletus luteus

Description: This mushroom grows from two to three inches in height, and the cap is from two to five inches across. The cap is convex and covered with a brownish separating gluten. Later it becomes yellowish-brown, streaked and spotted. The flesh is white; the tubes small and yellow when young; becoming darker with age. The stem is yellowish and dotted above the large, membranous brownish-white ring. It is yellowish or brownish-white below the ring. The stem is stout.

Where and When to Find It: The Sticky-Cap grows in pine woods and flourishes during the late summer and fall.

Comment: *Edible.* Because of its woodland habitat, woody trash sometimes clings to the glutinous cap, so each specimen should be carefully cleaned before placing it in the basket. It is of good texture and flavor, and is internationally known and relished. As with other glutinous or slimy species, it is best to remove the slime from the cap, peel off the tubes, and remove the stem before using.

Sticky-Stem Bolete
Boletus subluteus

Description: The Sticky-Stem Bolete so much resembles the Sticky-Cap that it is often mistaken for it. Its most distinguishing feature is that it is dotted both above and below the ring on the stem with reddish or brownish glandules. The ring is glutinous; at first concealing the tubes, then collapsing and forming a narrow whitish or brownish band around the stem. It is a little smaller in size than the Sticky-Cap and often the cap is nearly flat.

Where and When to Find It: The Sticky-Stem Bolete grows in the pine woods during summer and fall.

Comment: *Edible.* The flesh is tender, a trifle glutinous in texture, and of good flavor.

Yellow-Flesh Bolete
Boletus subaureus

Description: The cap of the Yellow-Flesh Bolete is convex or nearly flat; glutinous; pale yellow, sometimes having darker spots, and from two to four inches broad. In the young plant the margin is slightly woolly, this being of a grayish color. The flesh is a light yellow. The tubes are small or medium; more angular than in most species; growing down toward the stem.

The tubes are pale yellow in the young plant but become dingy and darker as the plant grows older.

The stem is stout, almost of equal width from top to bottom, has yellow dots both without and within, and is from one and a half to three inches long.

Where and When to Find It: This Bolete is very common in Oregon and Washington. It will stand a great deal of frost. In Crater Lake National Park, and in the Mount Hood National Forest, I have found specimens growing in late July and August, although elsewhere it seldom makes its appearance much before October. Possibly the altitude has something to do with its early appearance in these places. It grows where the timber is straggling and the ground more or less sandy.

Comment: *Edible.* The *subaureus* is a mushroom of excellent qualities and is plentiful. The tubes as well as the flesh are edible, cooking with the same evenness.

RUSTY BOLETE
Boletus granulatus

Description: This is another of our more common Boletes. The cap is two to four inches broad, convex, or nearly flat, glutinous, and of a rusty-brown color when moist; yellowish when dry. The flesh and short tubes are also yellowish, the latter growing closely into the stem. The stem, from one to three inches long, is stout and dotted with glandules above. It also has a yellowish tinge.

Where and When to Find It: The Rusty Bolete is common in the Northwest in coniferous woods, where it grows on the ground. It is a late-growing plant and can often be found in the fall after the frosts set in.

Comment: *Edible* and very good.

Yellow-Cap Bolete
Boletus bovinus

Description: The cap of *bovinus* is two to four inches in diameter, nearly flat, smooth, glutinous, and of a pale yellow color. The flesh is white. The tubes are very short, growing down on the stem. They are pale yellow or grayish in color when the plant is young, becoming rust-colored with age. The stem is usually the same thickness its full length, and colored like the top of the plant.

Where and When to Find It: The Yellow-Cap grows on the ground under pine and hemlock trees. It flourishes in late fall.

Comment: *Edible.* This species is tasty and has a good texture.

King Bolete
Boletus edulis

Description: Of this mushroom there are many varieties in our forests, and it is the most delicious of all the Boletes. The cap of the King Bolete grows from three to twelve inches in diameter, or even larger in some species. Once seen, and once eaten by the pot-hunter, he always searches for others of its kind. The conditions in which the King grows—the climate, altitude, soil, and density of the forest—often cause a difference in appearance and structure in the same species, and must be expected.

The descriptions which are typical, and from which the fungi can be recognized, are all that will be attempted here. Suffice it to say, the *edulis* is the best of all the Boletes. They are to be shunned only when found growing close to a fine specimen of a deadly Amanita. The spores of the Amanita have been known to contaminate mushrooms growing nearby. The spores can be carried by wind, or on the fur of passing rabbits or other animals.

The large cap is convex or nearly flat; smooth; moist; at first firm, then soft. It varies in color from grayish-red to brownish-red, or tawny-brown, and is often paler on the margin. The flesh is white or yellowish and reddish beneath the cuticle. The tubes are convex; nearly free and long. They are small, round, and white—then yellow to greenish. The stem is two to six inches long, straight or zigzag, slightly bulbous; white, pale, or brownish.

Where and When to Find It: The King Bolete grows in the woods on the ground and is usually found in summer.

Comment: *Edible.* This is one of the most highly prized Boletes gathered.

See color photograph 18.

CLUB-STEMMED BOLETE
Boletus edulis
variety, *clavipes*

Description: The Club-Stemmed Bolete is so closely related to the King, and so closely connected by the intermediate forms, that it seems to be only a variety of it, but one worthy of illustration.

The cap is four to six inches in diameter, fleshy, convex, bald, and grayish-red, bay-red, or chestnut-color. The flesh is white and unchangeable. The tubes, at first concave or nearly flat, are white and stuffed; then convex, slightly depressed around the stem and a yellow color. The stem is two to six inches long and one to one and one-half inches thick, tapering upward from an enlarged base; it is inversely club-shaped.

Boletus edulis
variety *clavipes*

Where and When to Find It: This *edulis,* the Club-Stemmed variety, grows in coniferous forests and in open places and is most plentiful in June and July. Specimens of this plant are plentiful in the Crater Lake region, but the hunter must be on the alert in order to gather them before the squirrels and deer eat them. In the vicinity of Mount Jefferson and Mount Hood the *edulis* grows to a very large size, weighing from six to fifteen pounds. The caps are waved, apparently with the weight of the tubes which seem to be so heavy that the top of the plant is handicapped in its upward growth. The *edulis* often grows up to eight inches in thickness.

Comment: *Edible.* The Club-Stemmed *edulis* is all good, unless the tubes have become watery, or worms have invaded the flesh. When the plant is young and fresh, the whole mushroom is delicious fried, broiled, or baked. These beefsteak mushrooms are a feast for the epicure as well as the hungry hunter.

TWO-COLORED BOLETE
Boletus bicolor

Description: The cap of the Two-Colored Bolete is two to six inches across, rounded, dry and firm, and dark red, becoming softer and paler in age and sometimes spotted or stained with yellow. The flesh of the cap is thick, pale, or distinctly yellow— often deep golden yellow after exposure. The stem is one to four inches long and approximately half an inch thick. Rarely is it one inch thick. The stem is solid and generally yellow at the top and red at the base. The stem flesh turns blue when wounded. The tubes are bright yellow or reddish-yellow, slowly changing to blue where wounded.

TWO-COLORED BOLETE
Boletus bicolor

Where and When to Find It: The Two-Colored Bolete grows singly and sometimes in small groups in the woods and on lawns in shaded areas.

Comment: *Edible* and good.

RED-STEMMED BOLETE
Boletus russelli

Description: This Red-Stemmed Bolete is easily distinguished by its stem, which is a red or burnt color; also by its dry, scale-like covering. The cap is thick, hemispherical, or rounded, and dry. The scales covering it are downy. It is yellowish underneath the scale-like hairs of the surface; sometimes cracked in areas. The flesh is yellowish and does not change when bruised or exposed to the air. The tubes are often depressed around the stem; rather large, and of a dingy-yellow or yellowish-red. The stem is often seven inches long, usually tapering upward, but sometimes equal. It is roughened by the margins of the reticular depressions.

RED-STEMMED BOLETE
Boletus russelli

Where and When to Find It: The Red-Stemmed Bolete grows in the woods, on the ground. It is most plentiful from June to September.

Comment: *Edible.* With this mushroom it is best to remove the tubes before cooking. It cooks soft, but is tasty. When raw, it is sweet and mild, and goes very well with a raw vegetable salad.

WHITE-CAP BOLETE
Boletus aestivalis

Description: The cap is from four to six inches broad, rounded, or nearly flat; even; smooth; of a whitish color. In dry weather it is covered with little grains. The flesh is yellow below, and white above. The tubes are nearly free from the stem and the mouths of the tubes are small, even, and yellow. The stem is from four to five inches long, thick, bulbous, and smooth. The stem is pale yellow in color, and within the base a sort of reddish color.

Where and When to Find It: The smooth White-Cap Bolete grows in the woods and in woodland pastures or fields. As its species name implies (from Latin *aestas,* summer), it is a summer-growing mushroom, plentiful from June to September.

Comment: *Edible.* The White-Cap is tasty, delicate in flavor, large and attractive, and altogether an interesting mushroom for the novice to seek.

CHESTNUT BOLETE
Boletus illudens

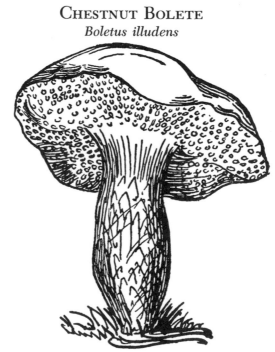

Description: The Chestnut Bolete has a rounded cap, dry or partly moist. The cap is chestnut color—yellowish-brown, sometimes tinged with red, which is deeper in color at the center. The flesh is dark cream or yellowish in color, and the tubes are a bright yellow, often larger near the stem. The stem is nearly equal, sometimes abruptly pointed at the base. It is smooth, pallid or yellowish, and has net-like markings at the top, or all over.

Where and When to Find It: The Chestnut Bolete grows in mixed woods, on the ground or an old stump. It is abundant in June and July.

Comment: *Edible.* This is another excellent mushroom—especially delicious when cooked like eggplant.

There are two Boletes that should not be gathered for food —not because they are harmful but because they are not palatable. The *Boletus felleus* is too bitter and the *Boletus pachypus* is nauseous. A brief description of these species follows.

BITTER BOLETE
Boletus felleus

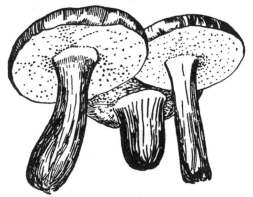

Description: The acrid taste of the *felleus*, or Bitter Bolete, is its worst offense. Aside from this, it is characterized at maturity by pink-like tubes, and the netted pattern on the upper portion of the stem. It is also to be identified by its brownish cap. The cap is rounded or nearly level, firm, becoming soft and smooth. The flesh is white, often changing to flesh color when the plant is wounded. The tubes are long and depressed around the stem, and joined. The tube mouths are angular and white at first, becoming tinged with pink later. The stem is variable, averaging from two to four inches long; equal or tapering upward—sometimes short, sometimes long; sometimes bulbous at the base. It is fairly smooth and colored like the cap, or paler.

Where and When to Find It: The Bitter Bolete is often found around decaying stumps in mixed woodlands, and it most commonly occurs in late summer.

Comment: The species is edible but not recommended because of the marked bitterness.

THICK-FOOTED BOLETE
Boletus pachypus

Description: This Thick-Footed little Bolete rises on a stem ranging from two to four inches; and it is noted for this thick, stout stem, which sometimes has a diameter of more than two inches. The stem is sometimes blood-red. At first it is bulbous, then elongated and equal. It is often variegated with red and pale yellow.

The cap is convex, brownish, or pale tan color; four to eight inches broad. The flesh is thick and whitish, changing slightly to blue. The tubes are rather long, somewhat depressed around the stem. Tube mouths are round, pale yellow, and tinged with green when old.

Where and When to Find It: This mushroom is found often in coniferous forests; it thrives in the late summer and early fall.

Comment: *Edible,* but not recommended because of its penetrating, unpleasant odor and somewhat nauseous flavor.

The Boletes, or Fleshy-Pore Mushrooms, constitute a large and varied group, but fleshiness they have in marked degree. Note the pleasingly plump edible varieties below—which suggest good eating later. To the left is a stump *edulis;* in the center is variety *areolatus* of the species *scaber;* and to the right is *pallidus*, pale but deliciously plump.

Stump *Boletus edulis*   *Boletus scaber—* variety *areolatus*   *Boletus pallidus*

Two species of Polypores that the pot-hunter will likely encounter in the woods are the Sulphur Polypore and the Hen-of-the-Woods, described below.

SULPHUR POLYPORE
Polyporus sulphureus

Description: This tufted Polypore, the Sulphur Mushroom, takes its name from the bright sulphur-yellow color of the pore layer. The upper surface varies from sulphur-yellow on the margin to a pinkish color toward the center. It grows in immense,conspicuous clusters or series of brackets or shelves from eight to twenty inches broad—the lower ones usually being the largest and the undersides crowded with round pores. Older shelves show radiating furrows and ridges that create a fan-like effect for the whole fruiting body. The sulphur-yellow of the young plant (occasionally even orange or reddish) changes to white with age. It is fleshy and watery when young, but punky with age. The flesh is white, yellow, or salmon color, and one-fourth to three-fourths inch thick.

Where and When to Find It: The Sulphur Polypore grows on either live or dead trees and stumps. It usually occurs in fall after rains, though in wet summers it may be quite abundant.

Comment: *Edible.* It is very good when young, but tough when mature or old.

See color photograph 19.

HEN-OF-THE-WOODS
Polyporus frondosus

Description: Hen-of-the-Woods Polypores grow in clusters from a common base; they are "tufted." The tufts sometimes are twelve inches across. The branches are numerous and up to two inches wide. The plant is dark gray to black on the upper surface, but on the under surface, or pore layer, it is white. It is wrinkled, lobed and intricately curved. The flesh is white, and the stems are also white, growing into each other. The pores are commonly round, but in an oblique position; gaping open and torn. The rough, lobed caps are fan shaped, or sometimes spoon shaped.

Where and When to Find It: Hen-of-the-Woods grows around the base of dead trees and stumps of deciduous trees. It is most abundant in wet seasons in August and September.

Comment: *Edible.* Hen-of-the-Woods is tender when young and the flavor is good, but tough when mature. Cook them well and cook them slowly.

SPINE MUSHROOMS *(Hydnums)*

Spine Mushrooms—sometimes called Tooth or Hedgehog Mushrooms—can be readily distinguished by the needle-like or icicle-like extensions which hang down from a cap or from a fleshy, shapeless mass of tissue. The spores are produced on the surface of the extensions or spines. In the Spine Mushrooms that have definite caps, the underside will have spines rather than gills. When there is no definite cap, the spines proceed from a fleshy mass and are larger. The spines invariably are pendent—they "hang."

Included here are three common species: Satyr's Beard, Medusa's Head, and the Coral Hydnum—all of them delicious and safe for the casual mushroom hunter.

Satyr's Beard
Hydnum erinaceum

Description: Satyr's Beard hangs in pendulous tufts, ranging from 2 to 10 inches across. The point of attachment is small, and the plant usually projects horizontally from the base. The tufts are white but change to a yellowish brown. The individual spines are crowded, slender, and tapering; generally 1 to 3 inches long.

Where and When to Find It: The *erinaceum* grows from crotches or wounds of trees, especially beach, oak, and locust, and can be found year after year in the same place. It has been found many times on the hardwoods of southern Oregon, and is a late summer and fall species.

Comment: *Edible* and delicious.

140

Satyr's Beard
Hydnum erinaceum
Edible

Medusa's Head
Hydnum caput-medusae

Description: The tufts of Medusa's Head hang from elms and oaks as a rule, and are often twenty inches across. First they are white, then gray. The body is compact; tapering to a solid base; which is more or less stem like. The spines cover the entire surface. Those upon the top are long, thin, and usually straight, while those around and toward the under side grow shorter.

Its name derives from the Greek legend of Medusa, the beautiful maiden whose hair was changed to serpents by the Goddess Athena.

Where and When to Find It: Medusa's Head grows on trees, usually from scars. It favors oaks or other hardwood species, and can be found in late summer and fall.

Comment: *Edible.* This is another of the tree-growing mushrooms that is delicious. While the whole plant is edible and excellent, the tender spines or teeth and more delicate parts are superb.

CORAL HYDNUM
Hydnum coralloides

Description: The Coral Hydnum cannot be mistaken for any other. It can be identified at a glance. It is from six to eighteen inches across, pure white and shining, but growing yellow with age. It is entirely composed of attenuated interlacing branches, one-half inch at the base, tapering to a point. The spines or teeth grow from one side of the branches; they are about one inch long and also taper to a point.

Where and When to Find It: The Coral Hydnum grows upon standing or fallen timber which is attacked by decay—as are the others upon which fungi usually grow. Fir, oak, beech, ash, birch, and other trees are inhabited by it, usually from August until frost.

Comment: *Edible.* Excellent.

See color photograph 20.

Mushrooms in Color

1. Fly Amanita—*Amanita muscaria*
2. False Morel—*Helvella infula*
3. White Lepiota—*Lepiota naucina*
4. Parasol Mushroom—*Lepiota procera*
5. Rodman's Mushroom—*Agaricus rodmani*
6. Fairy-Ring Mushroom—*Marasmius oreades*
7. Inky Cap—Coprinus *atramentarius*
8. Mica-Cap Coprinus—*Coprinus micaceus*
9. Delicious Lactarius—*Lactarius deliciosus*
10. Honey Mushroom—*Armillaria mellea*
11. Yellow Chanterelle—*Cantharellus cibarius*
12. Masked Tricholoma or Blewits—*Tricholoma personatum*
13. Giant Puffball—*Calvatia gigantea*
14. Half-Free Morel—*Morchella semilibera*
15. California Helvella—*Helvella californica*
16. Slate Helvella—*Helvella lacunosa*
17. Slippery Leotia—*Leotia lubrica*
18. King Bolete—*Boletus edulis*
19. Sulphur Polypore—*Polyporus sulphureus*
20. Coral Hydnum—*Hydnum coralloides*

Color Photographs © 1950 Sawyer's Inc., U. S. A.

Above:

1. Fly Amanita
Amanita muscaria
Poisonous

Below:

2. False Morel
Helvella infula
Poisonous

3.   White Lepiota
Lepiota naucina
Edible

4. Parasol Mushroom
Lepiota procera
Edible

5.   Rodman's Mushroom
Agaricus rodmani
Edible

6. Fairy-Ring Mushroom
Marasmius oreades
Edible

7. Inky Cap
Coprinus atramentarius
Edible

8. Mica-Cap Coprinus
Coprinus micaceus
Edible

Above:
9. Delicious Lactarius
Lactarius deliciosus
Edible

Below:
10. Honey Mushroom
Armillaria mellea
Edible

Above:
11. Yellow Chanterelle
Cantharellus cibarius
Edible

Below:
12. Masked Tricholoma
Tricholoma personatum
Edible

13.   Giant Puffball
Calvatia gigantea
Edible

14. Half-Free Morel
Morchella semilibera
Edible

15.   **California Helvella**
Helvella californica
Edible

16. Slate Helvella
Helvella lacunosa
Edible

17.   Slippery Leotia
Leotia lubrica
Edible

18.   King Bolete
Boletus edulis
Edible

Above:
19. Sulphur Polypore
Polyporus sulphureus
Edible

Below:
20. Coral Hydnum
Hydnum coralloides
Edible

Part III—Mushrooms as Food

SELECTION AND PREPARATION

Mushrooms should be cleaned as they are gathered. Trash and leaves should be brushed from them; the soiled base of the stems should be cut off, not only to remove adhering soil, but in order to see that the stems are free from worms; then the plants should be placed in the basket or paper sack, spore side down—in those of the gilled type.

When gathering mushrooms, it is best to place but one species in the same bag, unless species of about the same texture and flavor are found, and mixing is not objectionable.

If the mushrooms need washing, toss them lightly into a pan of water, rub them gently with the fingers; and after allowing the soil to settle, remove them from the water by passing the fingers under them and lifting them to the surface. Repeat this process until the mushrooms are free from soil. Some persons prefer to clean them with a brush, an excellent method.

It is seldom necessary to peel mushrooms, and it is generally not advisable to do so as most of the flavor is in the skin.

Though the stems of many species are quite edible, the stems of others may be rather tough. Be slow to discard the tough stems; they can be used very nicely in stews or soups.

If the mushrooms are not to be used till the next day, they can be preserved by boiling them about five minutes, draining and wiping them dry. It is best to cook them as soon as possible after gathering.

Many mushrooms mature and die in a day, as is true of the Inky Caps. If the mushrooms are not cooked when placed in the refrigerator, be sure to put them in a plastic bag or airtight container, to keep their natural moisture. Clean the raw ones but do not wash them before putting them in the refrigerator. Water will cause the mushrooms to degenerate sooner. Some hardy species of Agaricus will keep for several days in refrigeration, even in the raw state.

In estimating the amount to prepare, figure on one quarter pound per person, unless the mushrooms are the main part of the meal; then allow one half pound per person. Cooking oil— or even bacon drippings—may be used instead of butter in many of the following recipes. Margarine can always be substituted.

Canned or fresh mushrooms from your market, grocery store, or delicatessen, may be used instead of wild ones in most of these recipes. When purchasing fresh ones, select those that are firm and free from dark spots. Old, spotted, insect-eaten or water-logged plants should be avoided. All are highly perishable and best eaten the day they are gathered.

The kind of mushroom determines the best way of cooking it. Tough varieties require longer cooking time, while tender varieties should be cooked quickly. Some are bland, some spicy, some almost like beefsteak. The preferences of the eaters will also decide methods of cooking. Many prefer frying; others baking or stewing.

Seasoning also is a matter of individual taste. However, when in doubt, under-seasoning is preferable to over-seasoning. Too much seasoning can destroy the delicate taste of some species. Because many mushrooms—like the Chanterelles—shrink considerably in cooking, it is often better to season them shortly before they are done.

Mushrooms are a versatile food; they can be used in countless ways. They are good sliced raw in salads, stews and stuffings. Canned mushrooms enhance the flavor of buttered peas and green beans. Pour drained ones right into the vegetables. In gravy, stir canned mushrooms, liquid and all, into the mixture. In soups, mix undrained canned mushrooms or sliced fresh mushrooms; this is recommended for either canned or homemade soups. In stews or casseroles, add canned mushrooms during the last 20 minutes of cooking time.

Cooking time must usually be determined by the size and tenderness of the particular species and the amount of heat. If the mushrooms vary greatly in size it is a good idea to slice the larger specimens to balance cooking time. The art of mushroom cookery can be mastered with brief experience in trying out some of the suggested recipes included here.

The first section, Special Recipes, is adapted for use in cooking the fresh wild mushrooms. The second section, General Recipes, is for fresh mushrooms (wild or commercial) and also for canned mushrooms. For the most part, the recipes can be adjusted to either the canned or fresh, wild or commercial mushrooms. The character of the particular species is the best way to determine the type of preparation and cookery.

SPECIAL RECIPES
MEADOW MUSHROOMS (*Agaricus*)

Broiled Meadow Mushrooms

Remove stems and place caps on broiler, gills down; broil two minutes, turn and broil two minutes more. Season with salt, pepper and butter. Serve with bacon strips, or on toast.

Baked Meadow Mushrooms

Place whole mushrooms in a deep dish, on toast with scalded or clotted cream, or a little melted butter, and salt and pepper to taste. Cover and place in oven. The baking requires about a quarter of an hour at low heat, or before a fire. When mushrooms are taken up, do not remove the cover for a few minutes; by that time the vapor will have condensed and gone into the toast.

Meadow Mushrooms—Stewed on Toast

Cut the mushrooms—caps and stems—into pieces of equal size. Place in a covered saucepan. To each pint add two level tablespoonfuls of butter. Enough water will have been retained by the gills after washing to make sufficient liquid. Stew slowly twenty minutes; season to taste with pepper and salt. Serve on toast.

Fried Meadow Mushrooms

Lay mushrooms in a frying pan in which butter has been heated. Fry five minutes, place on hot dish. Pour over them a sauce made by thickening with a little flour the butter remaining in the pan. This is a delicious and simple way of cooking the plants, and it retains the mushroom's distinctive flavor. If the mushrooms vary greatly in size, it is advisable to slice the largest for uniform cooking.

Meadow Mushrooms Fricassee

Place one pound of mushrooms in a covered dish, sprinkle with a teaspoon of salt and a quarter of a teaspoonful of black pepper. Cover and cook slowly for five minutes. Moisten a tablespoonful of flour in half a cup of milk and strain this into the mushrooms. Bring to boiling point. Fold in the yolks of two eggs slightly beaten. Add a tablespoonful of chopped parsley, and serve at once.

BOLETES *(Boletus)*

Note: In cooking the Boletes or Pore Mushrooms, first always remove stems and tubes unless they are compact and young. Wipe the caps clean.

Broiled Boletes

Place caps in broiler or on a hot buttered pan. Cook well, usually about 4 minutes, depending on size of Boletes. If they are not fairly uniform, the larger ones should be sliced to equalize cooking time. Brush with melted butter; add salt and pepper; serve.

Stewed Boletes

Cut caps in pieces of similar size; stew slowly in own juices for about twenty minutes. Add water if necessary. When done, season. If there is sufficient liquid, thicken with flour, and add to the mushrooms when serving.

Baked Boletes

Bake in moderate oven in covered dish; add butter, parsley, a little garlic or onion if desired, pepper and salt.

Fried Boletes

Remove the tubes from the caps unless the plant is young, or of the short-tubed species. Slice the caps as you would eggplant. Fry in oil or butter, with or without at first dipping in batter or egg. Roll in crumbs or not, to suit your taste.

Apples or potatoes may be fried in the same pan while the mushrooms are cooking, flavor being added to each.

Boletus Edulis Soup—Hungarian

Dry the Boletes in a low oven. Soak in tepid water, thickening with toasted bread crumbs till the consistency is that of a puree. Then rub through a sieve. Add some stewed Boletes, boil together, and serve with seasoning to taste.

CHANTERELLES *(Cantharellus)*

Chanterelles may be prepared much like the Common Meadow Mushrooms, but care should be taken to prevent their exposure to great heat. Cook at low temperature and they will stay tender.

They are especially good when sliced across (after stems are removed) and stewed in gravy until tender. They are also recommended fried and placed on toast, or as the stuffing for toasted sandwiches.

CORAL MUSHROOMS *(Clavaria)*

Note: Coral Mushrooms may be cooked in any manner in which meats are prepared. To cook more quickly, it is best to shred the plant. Use only the tender parts for cooking, saving the tougher parts for drying and seasoning. This applies also to the tougher stems of some of the other varieties.

Fried Coral Mushrooms

Fry in hot butter or other fat or oil until well done. When tender, add milk or cream, thicken with flour, and season highly: always adding salt the last thing, as salt will toughen plants. They are also good stewed in a little water over low heat for half an hour.

INKY CAPS *(Coprinus)*

Note: All the Inky Caps should be cooked in a very low heat, and they must be covered or they lose their flavor.

Inky Caps—Creamed on Toast

Trim the stems and spread out the carefully cleaned mushrooms in a long baking dish. Dust lightly with salt and pepper. Dot with a few bits of butter. Cover and bake in a moderate oven for twenty-five minutes. Add four tablespoonfuls of cream; bring to boiling point; serve on toast.

SPINE MUSHROOMS *(Hydnum)*

Note: The Hydnums may be prepared the same way as the Chanterelles. If they seem tough, parboil for 5 minutes or so.

Sauteed Hydnums

Dice and dredge in flour and saute in butter. Add the seasoning (salt and pepper) just before serving as the Hydnums shrink considerably in cooking.

MILK MUSHROOMS *(Lactarius)*

Baked Delicious Lactarius

These juicy, delicious mushrooms are best baked at low heat. Place in baking dish, with salt, pepper and a bit of butter. Cover and bake for 40 to 45 minutes. Serve in the baking dish. They should be stewed for 35 to 40 minutes, but fried in much less time.

PARASOL MUSHROOMS *(Lepiota)*

Broiled Parasol Mushrooms

Clean as usual and remove the stems. Place the caps, gill side up, on a broiler. Baste them with melted butter and sprinkle with salt and pepper. Cook quickly for a moment; turn and cook quickly, gill side down. Serve in a heated serving dish or plate.

This recipe is excellent for all Lepiotas. They must be cooked rapidly to preserve their flavor and texture. They have thin flesh and broad gills. They are one of the best mushrooms for drying.

PUFFBALLS *(Lycoperdon, Bovistella, Calvatia)*

Fried Puffballs

No. 1—Remove the thin outer rind, slice, dip in egg and bread crumbs, and fry.

No. 2—Dice and fry.

No. 3—Dice and fry with diced potatoes.

No. 4—Dice fine, partly cook in hot fat, pour lightly beaten eggs over the mushrooms and scramble.

Stewed Puffballs

Cut in dice-shaped pieces, stew for fifteen minutes in a little water. Pour off water, dust with a little flour, add a small quantity of milk, butter, salt, pepper, and a little parsley. Stew slowly for five minutes. Serve.

Puffball Salads

Cut mushrooms into strips, mix with lettuce and watercress, or with dandelions, leeks and hard-boiled egg. Dress as usual for salad. Potato salad, with Puffballs added, served in lettuce shells is delicious. Fruit and Puffball combinations are dainty.

MORELS *(Morchella)*

Note: The Morels can be fried, baked, or stewed, according to the taste of the individual.

Morelles a l'Italienne

Slice the Morels across, and put on moderate heat, with some parsley, leek, chervil, burnet, tarragon, chives, a little salt, and two spoonfuls of fine oil. Stew till the juices run out, then thicken with a little flour. Serve with bread crumbs and a squeeze of lemon juice.

OYSTER MUSHROOMS *(Pleurotus)*

Note: Remove tough stem-parts, if any, and use only such parts of the plant as seem fresh and tender. Stew, fry, or bake, as you would oysters.

Fried Oyster Mushrooms

Cut into pieces about the size of a medium oyster, dip in egg and bread crumbs, and fry in hot butter or oil, as oysters are fried.

Oyster Mushrooms with cheese—au gratin

Cut into medium-sized pieces. Stew slowly, rather dry, for fiteen minutes. Pour off juice and save it. Place in baking dish (or in individual dishes, clam shells, etc.) a layer of oyster mushrooms, buttering and seasoning the layer. Sprinkle with bread crumbs and grated cheese. Repeat until dish is filled, placing cheese on top. Pour the juice over dish. Place in slow oven and bake until well browned.

Any mushroom may be cooked this way.

Oyster Mushroom Stew

Put into a saucepan a tablespoonful of butter or oil, add a clove of garlic, and a thin slice of onion; brown lightly and add a tablespoonful of flour. Mix, add a quarter of a teaspoonful of beef extract dissolved in half a cup of water and the same quantity of cream or evaporated milk. Bring to boiling point. Add a tablespoonful of chopped carrot, a bay leaf, and a blade of mace. Put the mixture on low heat and let simmer for ten minutes. Strain and add half a pound of oyster mushrooms. Cover and cook for another ten minutes. Serve on toast.

Coddled Oyster Mushrooms

To each half pound of mushrooms, add one rounded tablespoonful of butter in a saucepan. Sprinkle with salt to taste, cover dish, and cook slowly for five minutes. Beat the yolks of two eggs with one half cup of milk. Lift lid, add the mixture of eggs and milk. When smoking hot, serve. Do not allow mixture to come to a boil after the eggs are added, as it will become curdled.

MASKED TRICHOLOMA *(Tricholoma)*

Note: This species is good baked, broiled, or stewed.

Baked Tricholoma

Baked Tricholoma is especially delicious if prepared with a chicken or beef stuffing. Clean as usual, remove stems, place mushrooms on a baking dish, gill side up, and fill caps with stuffing. Cover and bake for 20 minutes.

GENERAL RECIPES

Mushrooms with Cheese

Several species of mushrooms are delicious when baked with a small quantity of cheese grated upon them; when several layers of mushrooms compose the dish, cheese should be grated upon each layer.

Mushroom Camp Bake

Cover the bottom of a tin plate with caps, spore surface up, sprinkle with salt and pepper, place a sliver of butter on each. Place another tin plate over all. Set on coals or a heated stone for fifteen minutes. Better baking will not result in the best oven.

Mushroom Croquettes

To two cups of any well-cooked mushroom of the meaty species, add two hardboiled eggs, a sprig of parsley, pepper, and salt. Chop all very fine, then add two level tablespoonfuls of butter and one of flour. Cook over low heat. Mix thoroughly, set aside to cool. When cold, shape, dip in egg and crumbs, and fry in hot oil, butter, or fat.

Deviled Mushrooms

Cut the mushrooms into small pieces, cook slowly until tender, adding butter, pepper, and salt. Let them cook almost dry, then add cream or milk and thickening. Add the yolks of two hardboiled eggs to each pint of meat, a pinch of red pepper, and a little chopped parsley. Serve hot or cold, nested in endive or lettuce.

Broiled Mushrooms I

After cleaning the mushrooms, remove stems. Dip the caps in milk or melted butter. Let stand one half hour. Place gills down, in greased broiler. Broil several minutes on each side. Sprinkle with salt and pepper and brush with melted butter. Serve on buttered dry toast, from which crusts have been removed.

With sausage: After turning mushrooms, fill with sausage meat, and broil until sausage is cooked.

Broiled Mushrooms II

Wash the mushrooms and remove the stems. Place the caps, gill side down, under the flame of the broiler for two or three minutes. Turn, sprinkle salt and pepper over the gill side, and place a small piece of butter in each cap. Broil under the flame a few minutes longer. Lift carefully from the broiler so that the juices are not lost.

Sauteed Mushrooms I

Slice crosswise one pound firm, clean mushrooms, and place in hot, buttered frying pan. If tough, peel and keep peel and stems for soup. Dredge with flour and cook 5 minutes. Pour on half cup of water. Cook 4 minutes. Sprinkle with parsley. Serve on dry toast.

Creamed. Use cream instead of water.

With Tomato. Use canned tomato soup instead of water.

Sauteed Mushrooms II

For one pound of mushrooms use 4 tablespoons of butter. Melt butter, add mushrooms, either sliced or whole, depending on size. Add salt, pepper and paprika. Cook on moderate heat. Stir occasionally.

This is a good sauce for meat if, before removing from heat, you sprinkle a tablespoon of flour over the mushrooms. Stir gently. Add half cup of sauterne. Cook till mixture thickens.

Creamed Mushrooms

1 pound mushrooms	1 cup rich milk or cream
Flour	Salt
2 tablespoons butter or other fat	Pepper

Wash the mushrooms and cut in half or into several pieces if they are large, slicing down through cap and stem. Flour the sliced mushrooms. Melt the fat, add the floured mushrooms, and brown delicately over moderate heat. As liquid cooks out of the mushrooms, pour it off and save it to add later.

When the mushrooms are well browned, pour in the milk or cream. Add the mushroom liquor and salt and pepper to taste. Stir and cook a few minutes longer to thicken. Serve on toast or biscuits.

Stuffed Mushrooms I

3 large mushrooms	Cream to moisten
2 tablespoons butter	½ teaspoon finely chopped
1 teaspoon finely	parsley
chopped onion	Salt, pepper, nutmeg
1 tablespoon flour	Buttered cracker crumbs

Remove stems and chop fine. Peel caps. Melt butter, add onion and chopped stems. Cook 10 minutes. Add flour, cream, and seasonings. Cool and fill caps with cooked chicken or ham or with mild cheese. Cover with buttered crumbs and bake 15 minutes in hot oven.

Stuffed Mushrooms II

1 pound large mushrooms (12 to 14)	2 cups fine bread crumps
4 tablespoons butter or other fat	2 teaspoons onion juice
	Pepper
¾ cup chopped celery	1 teaspoon salt
	1 tablespoon chopped parsley

Wash the mushrooms well, remove the stems close to the caps, and chop the stems fine. Melt 2 tablespoons of the fat, add the chopped mushroom stems and celery, cook for about 5 minutes. Stir in the bread crumbs and seasonings.

Turn the mushroom caps, gill side up, and fill them with mounds of the stuffing. Place the stuffed mushrooms in a shallow pan. Pour around them the rest of the melted fat and cover closely. Bake in a moderate oven (350° F.) for 30 to 45 minutes. Toward the last, remove the cover and let the crumbs brown lightly on top, or set the pan of mushrooms under the flame of the broiler a few minutes to brown.

Baked or Roasted Mushrooms

3 cups small mushroom caps   Salt and pepper
Butter   6 slices toast

Select mushrooms that are plump and small. Prepare caps and place, gill side up, in a baking dish. Sprinkle with salt and pepper and place a bit of butter in each cap. Set pan in a hot oven (425-450 F.) and cook for 15 minutes. The caps will be filled with their own liquor. Serve on toast, very hot.

Mushrooms Baked in Cream

Prepare 12 large mushrooms. Remove stems, peel caps. Place close together in a shallow buttered pan, cap side up. Season with salt and pepper, and dot with butter. Add ⅔ cup cream. Bake 10 minutes in a hot oven (425-450 F.). Place on dry toast rounds and pour over them remaining cream from pan.

Mushrooms with Bacon

Partially fry bacon, then add mushrooms and fry slowly till they are tender. The mushrooms take on the bacon seasoning and make a good morning relish.

Mushroom Meat Sauce

Canned or fresh mushrooms may be used. Wash fresh mushrooms, separate the caps from stems, trim the stems, and cut into pieces. Cook 1 pound mushrooms in 2 tablespoons butter in a pan five to ten minutes at moderate heat. Season and serve with beefsteak or other meat.

Canned Mushroom Sauce for Meats-Vegetables

Cook together, until a light brown, two tablespoonfuls each of butter and flour. Add a can of button mushrooms with liquid, and a cup of water or broth. Simmer five minutes, season and serve.

Fresh Mushroom Sauce for Meats-Vegetables

1 cup fresh mushrooms	2 teaspoons Worcestershire
1 cup cream sauce	sauce
1 tablespoon butter	1 teaspoon paprika

1 tablespoon cooking sherry

Fry the chopped mushrooms until slightly browned. Add to cream sauce and cook for ten minutes. Remove from fire and add remaining ingredients, stir, and serve with meats, vegetables—or omelette.

Brown Mushroom Sauce

3½ tablespoons butter	½ pound mushrooms, sliced
Few drops onion juice	1 teaspoon beef extract
3 tablespoons flour	Salt and paprika

1 cup cream (or rich milk)

Brown butter slightly, add onion juice and flour. Brown. Pour on cream gradually, while stirring constantly. Add mushrooms, sauteed in butter. Season with beef extract, salt, and paprika.

Sour Cream Sauce

Clean 1 pound mushrooms and, if large, slice. Put in a heavy pan with ½ cube of butter and 1 cup chopped onions. Cook slowly until the onions are soft. Blend in 2 tablespoons flour. Sprinkle with 2 teaspoons of paprika. Cook, stir for 4 minutes. Add 1 cup sour cream, and heat, do not boil. Serve on rice or baked white potatoes, or sweet potatoes.

Mushrooms with Mushroom Souffle

Select 12 large mushrooms (3 inches across) or 24 smaller ones. Remove and chop the stems. Cook the caps in butter for 5 minutes, turning once. Drain, cup side down, while mixing the souffle. Saute the stems in butter for 10 minutes. Add 2 tablespoons butter and blend in 3 tablespoons flour. Gradually stir in ¾ cup cream and cook, stirring, until thick. Add salt, pepper, and 1 teaspoon tarragon. Remove from heat and add a few drops vinegar. Beat in slowly the yolks of 4 eggs. Beat the 4 egg whites until stiff, and fold in the mixture. Place the drained mushroom caps (cup sides up) in even rows in a greased baking dish. Pour in the souffle mixture, heaping it up over mushroom caps. Bake in a moderate oven (about 350 F.) about 20 minutes—until lightly brown. To serve, cut through between the mushrooms and lift out 2 or more mushrooms for each serving.

Old-Fashioned Mushroom Soup

Almost any kind of edible mushroom can be used in making soup. Add one quart of mushrooms to three pints of water. Boil slowly for one hour in covered pan. Rub the whole through a sieve. Add one-half pint of milk, thickened with one tablespoonful of flour; one rounded tablespoonful of butter, salt and pepper, and a sliver of bay leaf. Bring to a boil, and serve.

Cream of Mushroom Soup I

1 pound mushrooms	1 cup cream
¼ cup melted butter	Salt
4 tablespoons flour	Pepper
1 quart milk	Finely chopped parsley
2 slices onion	

Wash and skin the mushrooms. Chop them fine and brown about 10 minutes in 2 tablespoons of the butter. Mix the flour with a little of the cold milk until smooth. Heat the remaining milk in a double boiler, with the onion. Mix a little of the hot milk with the milk and flour mixture. Then stir this mixture into the hot milk and cook until thickened. Add the rest of the butter, cover and cook about 5 minutes longer. Remove the onion, stir in the mushrooms and cream. Season with salt and pepper. Serve with chopped parsley over the top.

Cream of Mushroom Soup II

½ pound mushrooms   3 pints consomme   Sherry

Clean mushrooms, chop stems finely and break caps in small pieces. Add mushrooms to consomme, bring slowly to boiling point. Simmer 25 minutes. Strain through moistened double-thickness cheesecloth. Re-heat. Just before serving add sherry to taste. Serves 8.

Mushroom Puree

¼ pound mushrooms   1 cup consomme
2 tablespoons butter   1 tablespoon flour
Salt and pepper

Clean mushrooms, break in pieces, and cook 5 minutes in 1 tablespoon butter. Add consomme; simmer 5 minutes. Rub through sieve and add remaining butter and flour cooked together. Season with salt and pepper.

Scrambled Eggs with Mushrooms

Slice a cup of fresh mushrooms and cook in 2 tablespoons of butter about 5 minutes. Season with salt and pepper. Stir in slightly beaten eggs and scramble. (Drained canned mushrooms can also be used.)

Mushroom Omelet

Saute 1 cup chopped mushrooms in 3 tablespoons butter or margarine. Lightly season with salt and pepper. Place on half the omelet, fold over other half of omelet, covering the mushroom filling.

Mushrooms on Toast

Prepare mushrooms and place in greased baking dish, cap side down. Dot with butter. Season with salt and pepper. Pour ¾ cup light cream over mushrooms. Place in hot oven for 10-15 minutes. Place mushrooms on buttered toast. Pour cream remaining in baking dish over the mushrooms and toast.

Mushroom Sandwich Filling

Chop ½ pound mushrooms (caps and stems) very fine. Mince 5 small green onions and cook until tender in 3 tablespoons butter. Add the chopped mushrooms, cover, and cook slowly for 10 minutes. Add 1 tablespoon flour; salt and pepper to taste. Stir in ½ cup cream. Cook and stir for 5 minutes, or until very thick. Cool before using on sandwiches. Mixed with 1 cup of canned beef gravy (and heated), this filling makes an excellent meat or vegetable sauce.

Broiled Mushrooms Flambe

To dramatize a steak, serve it with mushrooms broiled on skewers, and flamed.

Prepare 1½ pounds medium-size, uniform mushroom caps (save stems for soup). Impale the caps on four skewers. Brush with melted butter, season with salt and pepper. Cook over charcoal or under broiler, turning to brown on all sides. Baste twice with butter. Broil till tender—about 10 minutes. Arrange mushrooms on a hot fireproof dish and pour over them 3 tablespoons warmed Cognac. When flames die, serve with steak. Serves 4.

Marinated Mushrooms I

1 pound small mushrooms   ½ cup French dressing
2 tablespoons olive oil   1 clove garlic cut in half

Lightly brown mushrooms in olive oil. Cover with French dressing, add garlic. Let stand over night in refrigerator. These may be used as appetizers or in salads.

Marinated Mushrooms II

Clean and slice 1 pound uniform mushrooms, slicing right through stem and cap. Mix ¾ cup olive oil, 3 tablespoons tarragon vinegar, salt, pepper, minced parsley, and ½ teaspoon minced tarragon. Stir well and let stand 5 hours at room temperature. Use as appetizers or in salad.

Mushroom Butter

Saute a quarter pound of finely chopped mushrooms in 2 tablespoons of butter for 5 minutes. Add 2 teaspoons of sherry, ½ cube butter, salt and pepper to taste. Cream together. If you wish, add a little garlic (about half a small clove) or a pinch of minced tarragon. This butter is excellent on steaks or broiled fish, or as a spread for chicken breast sandwiches.

Mushroom Canapes

Slice whole large mushrooms vertically, right through the stem. Place in a heavy saucepan (4 large mushrooms will give you 15 to 20 slices). Sprinkle with salt and cover lightly with cream. Place over high heat. As soon as the cream boils, turn the heat to low and cook, stirring occasionally, until the cream is thick and browned. Place mixture in a chafing dish and keep hot. For each canape, put a slice of mushroom, covered with brown cream, on a round of toast right before serving.

Mushroom Pates

Prepare the plants as for deviled mushrooms (See page 170), fill pastry shells while the mixture is hot, and serve. Shells may be decorated daintily by dipping the rims of the shells in partially beaten egg white, then in finely-chopped parsley before filling.

Mushroom Cheese Sauce

1 can condensed cream of mushroom soup	¾ cup shredded cheese ⅛ teaspoon pepper

Combine soup and cheese. Heat slowly. Add pepper. Serve on rice or almost any vegetable.

Mushroom Tomato Sauce I

2½ tablespoons chopped bacon
   (or raw ham)
5 slices carrot
Piece of bay leaf
2 sprigs thyme
Sprig of parsley
1 small slice onion

Few gratings nutmeg
3 tablespoons flour
2 cups tomatoes
1½ cups Brown Stock
Salt and pepper
1 cup mushrooms,
   cut in quarters

2 cloves

Cook bacon, onion, and carrot 5 minutes; add bay leaf, thyme, parsley, cloves, nutmeg, and tomatoes, and cook another 5 minutes. Add flour moistened with enough cold water to pour. As sauce thickens, thin with stock. Cover and cook in oven 1 hour. Strain. Add salt and pepper to taste, and mushrooms. Cook 5 minutes. For quick brown stock, use bouillon cubes or beef extract, dissolved in water; or canned consomme or bouillon.

Mushroom Tomato Sauce II

¼ cup shortening
1 can (4 ounces) mushrooms

1 8-ounce can tomato sauce
1 small onion, minced

Melt shortening in saucepan. Brown mushrooms and onion slowly, about 5 minutes. Add liquid from mushrooms and tomato sauce. Simmer, uncovered, about 10 minutes.

Mushroom Stuffing I

Saute 2 pounds sliced mushrooms and one large onion in a cup of butter for 5 minutes. Add 4 sliced celery stalks, ¼ cup minced parsley, 2 teaspoons tarragon, 1 teaspoon salt, and a little pepper. Cool 5 minutes, then add another half cup of butter. Stir into 10 cups toast crumbs. Mix well, add salt to taste, and just enough water to moisten. Test by squeezing a handful, then opening the fingers. The stuffing should partially hold its form and not be soggy. This amount of stuffing is sufficient for a 12 to 14-pound turkey.

Mushroom Stuffing II

1 cup mushrooms, cut in
   pieces
½ cup butter
Salt and pepper
1½ cups bread crumbs

Saute mushrooms in butter and add other ingredients. Makes 2 cups of stuffing.

Mushroom and Egg Stuffing

½ pound mushrooms, sliced,
   and sauteed in butter
2½ cups bread crumbs
Stock or water to moisten
1 hard-boiled egg, chopped
2-inch cube fat salt pork,
   finely chopped
Salt and pepper
¼ teaspoon poultry seasoning, if liked

When making enough for 10-12 pound turkey, use 10-12 cups bread and add 1 beaten egg. Makes 4 cups of stuffing.

Spicy Mushroom Stuffing

1 cup finely chopped mushrooms, sauteed in butter
Few drops onion juice
1 cup toast crumbs
Salt, pepper, celery salt
Few grains cayenne and nutmeg
½ teaspoon chopped chives
2 tablespoons melted butter
½ cup stock or water
½ tablespoon chopped parsley

Mix and season to taste. Makes between 2 and 3 cups of stuffing.

Cocktail Mushrooms

Prepare ½ pound attractive small mushrooms. Remove skins and stems. Cover with sherry and soak 2 to 3 hours. Drain, fill with seasoned lobster paste, Roquefort or caviare. Serve on toothpicks or cocktail sticks.

Mushroom Canape Spread

Chop ½ pound mushrooms fine, saute in butter, sprinkle with flour, add heavy cream to make thick paste. Season (with brandy, if preferred). This is delicious with toasted or rolled sandwiches.

Rolled Sandwiches I

Cut thin slices of white, fine-grained bread. Remove crust if preferred. Spread with mushroom filling. Roll, fasten with toothpicks, and chill. Remove toothpicks before serving. Garnish· with parsley. Rolled sandwiches are excellent toasted. Cut in half if desired.

Rolled Sandwiches II

Cut slices lengthwise of loaf. Remove crust if preferred. Spread with mushroom filling. Roll and wrap tightly in dry towel, then in moist one, and chill. When ready to serve, cut in thin slices.

Toasted Mushroom Sandwiches

Chop mushrooms, dredge lightly with flour, saute in butter, and moisten with cream. Season with salt, pepper, nutmeg and paprika. Spread sandwiches with mushroom filling. Brush with melted butter and toast in broiler or saute in butter in heavy fry pan.

Baked Haddock with Mushrooms

2 haddock fillets	Mushroom stuffing
½ cup sauteed bread crumbs	⅔ cup cream or milk
2 tablespoons lemon juice	Salt and pepper

Brush fish with lemon juice and season with salt and pepper. Put one fillet in greased pan, spread with stuffing, cover with other fillet, pour over cream or milk, and bake 25 to 30 minutes in moderate oven. Sprinkle with bread crumbs and bake until crumbs are brown. Place on serving dish and pour over remaining liquid. Serves 5 or 6.

Stuffing: Mix ½ cup bread crumbs with 3 tablespoons melted butter and ½ cup chopped mushroom caps, salt and pepper to taste.

Beefsteak Smothered in Mushrooms

Prepare two cupfuls of Meadow or Milk Mushrooms. Add salt, pepper and butter and bake till tender. Broil the steak until it is almost done. Place it in the pan with the

mushrooms (put some of the mushrooms on top of the steak).
Return to oven for 5 to 10 minutes. Serve.

Sweetbread and Mushroom Timbales

3 tablespoons butter
1 sliced onion
2 cups chopped mushrooms
1 medium-sized sweetbread,
  parboiled and chopped
1 cup white sauce

⅓ cup stale bread or toast
  crumbs
½ teaspoon salt
2 egg yolks, well beaten
2 egg whites, beaten stiff
Mushroom sauce

1 chopped red pepper

Cook butter and onion 5 minutes. Add remaining ingredients. Bake. Serve with Mushroom Sauce. Makes 12 to 14 molds.

Chicken with Mushrooms

1 3-pound cut-up chicken
1 pint buttermilk
⅔ cup flour
1 teaspoon salt
½ teaspoon paprika

¼ teaspoon pepper
4 ounces of dried mushrooms
  or dried mushroom soup
1 cup water
½ cup oil

Soak the pieces of chicken in buttermilk overnight or several hours. To cook, remove chicken pieces from buttermilk and roll them in the mixed dry ingredients. Brown in oil. Mix mushrooms and water, pour over chicken. Bake in 350-degree oven about one hour. Serves 3 or 4.

Chicken a la King

4 tablespoons butter
2 tablespoons flour
1 cup milk
1 cup cream
1 teaspoon salt
⅛ teaspoon pepper

½ green pepper, chopped
1 cup mushrooms,
  cut in pieces
2 cups cooked diced chicken
1 chopped pimiento,
  and juice

2 egg yolks

Make a white sauce using 3 tablespoons of fat, the flour, milk, cream, salt, and pepper. Melt the rest of the butter in a frying pan, add the green pepper and the mushrooms, and cook for a few minutes over low heat. Beat the egg yolks, stir a small quantity of the white sauce into them and add them to the rest of the sauce. Add the other ingredients and cook until the mixture is heated thoroughly. Serve in patty shells or on crisp toast.

Green Beans with Mushrooms

1 can (No. 2 size) French-cut green beans   6 ounces sliced mushroom caps

1 medium onion cut in rings

Place all ingredients in casserole, mix and bake 1½ hours in 350-degree oven.

20-Minute Casserole

1 can luncheon meat   1 cup chopped mushrooms
1½ cups sliced cooked potatoes   1 cup bouillon

Cut luncheon meat into slices and each slice into quarters. Arrange alternate layers of meat and potatoes in a greased 1-quart baking dish. Cover with mushrooms and bouillon. Bake in a moderate oven (350 F.) 20 minutes, or until top bubbles. Makes 4 servings.

Shepherd's Mushroom Pie

1 cup small mushrooms   1½ cups diced left-over meat
¼ cup water   1½ cups mashed potatoes

1 cup bouillon or brown gravy

Mix mushrooms in bouillon or gravy, water and meat. Pour into 1 quart baking dish. Spread mashed potatoes over top.

Bake in moderate oven 20 minutes, or until potatoes are lightly browned. Makes 3 servings.

Mushroom Chow Mein

1 large can mushrooms   1½ cups shredded celery
1½ pounds shredded pork   1 tablespoon molasses
¼ cup salad oil   2½ tablespoons soy sauce
1½ cups minced onion   1 package Chinese noodles

3¼ cups bean sprouts

Fry pork 30 minutes at medium heat in salad oil, and add onions. After 5 minutes add bean sprouts, celery and mushrooms. Cook 10 minutes and add molasses and soy sauce. Cook 2 minutes. Serve over noodles that have been parboiled in salted water for five minutes and drained well. Serves 5 people.

Mashed Potatoes with Mushrooms

Peel 4 medium-sized potatoes and cook, with a peeled clove of garlic, in slightly salted water to cover. When potatoes are tender, drain. Remove the garlic; mash the potatoes. Add ½ cup light cream, and season to taste. Saute 1½ cups sliced mushrooms in butter; add to the potatoes. Mix well and place in a greased casserole dish. Dot with butter and brown and heat in the oven. Makes 4 servings. (Note: Commercially prepared mashed potatoes may be substituted.)

Pickled Mushrooms—English

Take button mushrooms (Puffballs may be used) and remove rough ends only. Put into jars and cover with cold, spiced pickling vinegar. Add a few small red peppercorns and mustard seeds and seal.

DRYING MUSHROOMS

Mushrooms can be dried and successfully kept for at least a year. They must be kept dry, though, and free from insects. If exposed to moisture or high humidity, dried mushrooms, like dried vegetables, deteriorate quickly.

The best method of drying is by placing them on a wire rack in a current of warm air. If the temperature is raised to 130 degrees Fahrenheit for a few hours, any insects infesting the mushrooms will be destroyed. However, dry the plants as quickly as possible, without burning; and complete the process once it is started.

Especially large or moist species will dry faster if sliced. Since they are 50 to 90 per cent water, there is considerable shrinkage. Ten pounds of fresh mushrooms will often shrink in weight to about one pound of dried ones. This makes storage easy.

Sun drying is possible but ordinarily it will need to be combined with artificial drying.

A traditional method of drying is by placing the mushrooms on paper in a moderate oven; then putting them in paper bags and hanging them in a dry place until required for use. Whatever method used, it is important to label the containers.

The dried mushrooms are handy and delicious seasoning.

A slight variation in drying can be had by the following method:

Mushroom Flakes

Grate or thinly slice fresh mushrooms, preferably Puffballs or other firm-fleshed species. Spread the flakes or slices in the sun to dry, or in a warm oven. When thoroughly dry, place in sealed jars and use for seasoning.

FREEZING MUSHROOMS

Mushrooms will keep for a considerable time if they are blanched by steaming or boiling before freezing. Blanching will take around 4 minutes, in most cases. If the mushrooms are frozen in the raw state, they will retain their full flavor and texture for only about a month.

MUSHROOMS, A SURVIVAL FOOD

Should you become lost—or forced from familiar surroundings by disaster—survival would make four demands. Above all else, the survivor needs to be as calm as possible so that he will be better able to discover the essentials of water, food, and shelter. Of these, shelter is usually the easiest to arrange. It can be found under the low-hanging branches of a stand of firs, or under a rock shelf. Caves, hollow trees, trenches, and bushes— all these provide adequate shelter under certain conditions.

Beyond composure, water is the main need for survival. Water may not always appear as a bubbling spring or a clear, flowing stream; it can often be found in a pond covered with algae, in animal tracks, or in some muddy puddle. In these latter cases the water should be boiled or otherwise purified, to avoid the risk of disease.

A source of water that few consider is the sap of most plants found in the temperate climates, also the juices of the fleshy fruits. Mushrooms growing in the fields or on decaying logs or trees contain from fifty to ninety per cent water—as high a percentage as in watermelons. Like other fruits, mushrooms provide some food value, as well as water, thus satisfying two urgent needs.

Water may also be secured from dew, fog, or other precipitation, by laying a piece of plastic on the ground and directing the moisture into a container. Many large leaves that have been overlaid like shingles will serve in place of the plastic. The container could be one that was brought along, or one improvised from materials at hand, such as a hollowed rock or even a hat. Water is not so difficult to secure as is usually believed, but its many sources are often overlooked.

Survival is possible for many days without food, yet not nearly so many without water. Just how much water is needed depends on the person and the climatic conditions.

Prospects for food may look bleak because none of the everyday foods appear in the form in which they are normally served at home. There are, though, usually plenty of foods available to prevent starvation. The plant kingdom of the world is made up of more than 300,000 species, besides the myriad varieties; and the animal kingdom is composed of more than 800,000 species. This adds up to more than a million species, most of which are edible, and many of which will likely be present wherever the survivor is.

Midsummer generally offers the greatest variety of available food, both plant and animal, though, regardless of locality, all four seasons provide an abundance. Winter, however, requires a little more resourcefulness in the survivor. Plant foods, rather than animals foods, will likely constitute a major part of the survivor's diet because they are more plentiful and more easily obtained without equipment. Besides, they are usually rich in vitamins and often require no cooking. By far the greatest number of wild plants are edible. As a rule, plants which resemble the familiar, cultivated ones should be selected. Bamboo sprouts resemble asparagus, wild onions look and smell like scallions, mangoes are similar to pears, and so on. This is the surest way to find edible and nourishing plant foods.

Mushrooms are one of the best survival foods available, not only because of their abundance but because the many edible ones can easily become recognizable through use of such a book as this volume. When collected for survival food, they can be eaten raw or cooked as they would be eaten at home—if a fire is possible. Boiling will furnish liquid nutrition from the mushrooms, even if the flesh is too tough to be eaten. Though mushrooms are low in starch, protein, and other substances useful as food, they are a good source of vitamins and minerals, such as copper and iron, and have some fuel value.

Poisonous mushrooms are generally varieties of the Amanita. They have a frill or ring or "veil" around the upper part of the stalk, plus a "volva" or cup at the base into which the stalk fits. This volva is usually just below ground level or is covered by dead leaves and twigs. Edible mushrooms sometimes have the veil but never the volva. In picking young mushrooms, don't mistake young Amanitas (poisonous) for young Puffballs. Cut the young "button" vertically. If you find gills or a cup, discard the sample. Only solid white flesh is found in the Puffball. Young Amanitas have all the characteristics of a mature mushroom—although reduced and compressed—while the Puffball does not. When the button or young plant is too small to be firm, do not eat it.

However, don't take for granted that all mushrooms with gills are poisonous. Most mushrooms with gills are edible. The nonedible mushrooms usually have white spores which will drop from the gills when the mushroom is tapped.

Morels, coral fungi, pore fungi, coral hydnums, and cup fungi are all edible. This group includes those with conical, honeycomb-like caps, those with a sponge-like look, and those that look like coral. These kinds are generally found in wooded areas on the ground, or on dead trees.

In this same wooded area is another historic source of food, immediately obtainable. You may eat the inner bark of many trees, raw or cooked. In famine areas, people make flour from the inner bark of trees. The thin, green, outer bark and the white, innermost bark are the parts normally used for food, since brown bark ordinarily contains bitter tannin. Among those trees whose bark is used as a source of food are the poplars (including cottonwoods and aspens), birches, and willows. The inner bark and growing tips of a few species of pine can be eaten. Pine bark is especially valuable for vitamin C. The outer bark of these pines is scraped away and the inner bark stripped from the trunk and consumed, fresh, dried, or cooked. Bark is most palatable when newly formed in the spring.

Many trees of the pine family contain edible saps which have a useful sugar content. One of these is the sugar pine of the West Coast. Another such tree is the balsam fir, which is found from the northern United States well up into Canada. The sap of the sugar maple may be boiled down to make maple sirup and maple sugar. The best sap is obtained between February and April.

All four seasons of the year provide the reliable and tasty mushroom. In the spring, a wide variety supplies both food and water. Except for the arid or desert areas, most places have the same abundance of mushrooms in the summer. In the fall, a good collection is still available. Many of these fall species are often available till the first frost or even throughout a moderate winter. However, mushrooms occur mainly in the mild coastal areas during the winter season, except for fully mature ones that remain from the fall crop.

GLOSSARY

ANNULUS—Remnants of the veil useful in the identification of certain mushrooms. See "Ring."

APEX—The tip of the part described.

APPRESSED—Pressed closely to body to which attached.

ATTENUATED—Having a very slender prolongation at the tip.

BAY-BROWN—A reddish-brown.

BULBOUS—Having an oval or abrupt enlargement, or bulb, at the base.

CAP—The umbrella-like expansion on the apex of the stalk in a mushroom. It bears the gills, teeth, or pores on the underside. "Pileus" is the technical term applied to it.

COMPRESSED—Flattened, especially laterally or from side to side.

CONCAVE—Curved like the inside of a sphere or globe.

CONCENTRIC—Having a common center, as circles or spheres, but each succeeding circle either large or smaller in diameter that the preceding.

CONICAL—Cone-shaped.

CONIFEROUS—Bearing cones, as the pine or fir or cypress.

CONVERGENT—Tending to come together at a point.

CONVEX—Rounded or regularly elevated toward the center like an inverted bowl (used to describe the cap of certain mushrooms).

CUP—The scales or sheath seen at the base of the stalk in some mushrooms. The cup is the remnant of a structure which completely covers the developing mushroom at first, but is ultimately broken and left at the base, usually partly underground. See "Volva."

CUTICLE—The differentiated surface layer (not typical of all species).

DECIDUOUS—Said of trees or shrubs that shed their leaves in the fall.

DEFLEXED—Bent sharply downward.

DEPRESSED—With the central part sunken below the margins (said of a cap).

DICHOTOMOUS—Repeatedly forking into two equal branches.

DILATED—Enlarged or swollen.

DISK—The central part of the surface of the cap, roughly halfway to the cap margin.

EXPANDED—Completely spread out (said of a cap).

FETID—Disagreeable, repulsive (refers to odor).

FIBRILLOSE—Covered with appressed hairs or threads, more or less evenly disposed. See "Appressed."

FIBROUS—Composed of tough, stringy tissue.

FLESH—Inner substance of the stem or cap, exclusive of the external layer, and of gills, teeth, or pores.

FLEXUOUS—Zigzag; bent at the nodes or joints.

FREE—Not attached to the stalk at any time during development (refers to gills).

FURROWS—Narrow grooves.

GELATINOUS—Jelly-like in consistency.

GENUS—The first major grouping above the rank of species (plural: genera).

GILLS—The knifeblade-like, radially-arranged plates of tissue on the underside of a mushroom cap. "Lamellae" is the technical term. See "Teeth" and "Tubes."

GLANDS (GLANDULES)—Usually small structures secreting some definite substance. A gland may be at the tip of a hair, on the surface of a leaf or stalk, or imbedded in the tissue.

GLOBOSE—Globular, spherical.

GLUTINOUS—Slimy or sticky.

GRAINS—Tiny solid particles, as sand.

GRANULES—Grains or grain-like particles.

GREGARIOUS—Growing in groups, but separate at the base.

HEMISPHERICAL—Shaped like half a sphere or globe.

INK—A dark liquid secretion caused by the self-digestion of the tissue.

INVOLUTE—Rolled in from the margin.

LAMELLAE—Gills of a mushroom.

LATERAL—Attached to one side of the cap (to describe the stem).

LIVID—Grayish-blue, as the color caused by bruising.

LOBE—A prominence set off by more or less deep indentations.

MARGINATE—Having a distinct margin.

MEALY—Covered with fine granules.

MELTING—Disappearing gradually.

MEMBRANOUS—Thin, membrane-like.

MINUTE—Very small, tiny.

MOUTH—The tissue around the opening of the tube on the underside of the mushroom cap.

NAKED—Devoid of any type of covering (to describe a stem or cap).

NOTCHED—With a V-shape cut in the margin.

OBLIQUE—Having the sides unsymmetrical.

OBOVOID—Egg-shaped, with the broad end toward the apex. Inversely ovoid.

OBTUSE—Blunt, not pointed.

OVATE—Shaped like a longitudinal section through a chicken egg.

OVOID—Egg-shaped, in the exact sense.

PALLID—Very pale; used alone, it means off-white.

PARTIAL VEIL—The inner veil which extends from the margin of the cap to the stem and at first covers the gills or pores.

PERIDIUM—The outer coat of the spore-bearing mushrooms, as in puffballs.

PILEUS—Technical term for mushroom cap.

PIT—A small depression on the surface.

PLANE—Flat.

PLATES—Thin, flat layers of tissue.

PLIANT—Flexible.

PORES—The tiny holes in the tissue layer on the under surface of the cap of pore mushrooms.

RADIAL—Spreading or branching out in all directions from a common center.

REFLEXED—Sharply bent back.

RETICULATE—Marked with cross lines like the meshes of a net.

RIBBED—Appearing as the veins of a leaf.

RING—The ring of tissue left on the stalk from the breaking of the partial veil. See "Annulus."

SCALES—Torn portions of cuticle or veil. Usually these remnants are arranged in some sort of pattern.

SHAGGY—Having a rough surface.

SPECIES—A group of plants or animals having one or more characteristics in common. See "Genus."

SPINDLE-SHAPED—Gradually tapering from center toward both ends.

SPORES—The tiny reproductive bodies of mushrooms.

STEM (STALK)—The part of the mushroom differentiated as a supporting structure for the cap. It is not present on all mushrooms with caps, but in those cases the log or material the cap grows on serves the purpose.

STUFFED—Having the axis or interior of the stem filled with a distinctly different material than outer layer, usually softer, such as pith, which may break down in age, leaving a hollow.

SUBGLOBOSE—Nearly globular or spherical.

SUPERIOR—Attached above the middle of the stalk (referring to the ring).

TAWNY—About the color of a lion.

TEETH—Thorn-like or spine-like structures on the undersurface of the cap or branches of the Hydnums.

TOOTHED—Notched or indented.

TRANSLUCENT—Appears partially transparent.

TRANSVERSE—Crosswise.

TRUNK—The main stalk of a tree or plant.

TUBES—Tubular or pipe-like structures found in the caps of the polypores and boletes. Seen only when the cap is cut through.

TUFTED—Formed as a cluster or bunch attached together at the base.

UNIVERSAL VEIL—The veil which envelops the young fruiting body in some species. It is the outer layer of tissue distinct from cap and stem.

VOLVA—The remains of the universal veil left around the base of the mushroom after the veil has broken.

WARTS—Small pieces of universal-veil tissue (on a cap).

INDEX

A

Agaricus (Agarics), description of, 32 ff. (*See* Meadow Mushrooms)
Agaricus: *arvensis*, 41; *californicus*, 40; *campestris*, 36; *elvensis*, 39; *foederatus*, 38; *magnificus*, 41; *maritimus*, 38; *placomyces*, 43; *rodmani*, 37
Amanita: *mappa*, 18, 21; *muscaria*, 18; variety *formosa*, 20; variety *regalis*, 20; variety *umbrina*, 20; *phalloides*, 17; *verna*, 19, 29; *virosa*, 18, 19
Amanitas (*Amanita*): description of, 12 ff.; place of growth, 15, 22; comparison with Lepiotas, 22, 26, 27, 28; confusion with Meadow or Field Mushrooms, 32, 40; comparison with Pore Mushrooms, 120
American Lepiota, 29
Amethyst Coral, 112
Armillaria mellea, 67
Asci, 104
Ash-Colored Coprinus, 56
Atlantic (ocean), 110

B

Bell Mushroom, 38
Bitter Bolete, 135
Blewits Mushroom, 72
Boletes, description of, 120 (*See* Pore Mushrooms)
Boletus: *aestivalis*, 133; *bicolor*, 131; *bovinus*, 129; *eastwoodiae*, 125; *edulis*, 129; variety *clavipes*, 130; *felleus*, 135; *granulatus*, 128; *illudens*, 134; *luteus*, 126; *pachypus*, 135; *pallidus*, 137; *russelli*, 132; *scaber*, 125; variety *areolatus*, 137; *subaureus*, 127; *subluteus*, 127
Bovistella, description of, 78, (*See* Puffballs)
Bovistella ohiensis, 92
Brain Mushroom, 106
Broad-Based Puffball, 92
Brown Gyromitra, 108
Bulbous Agaricus, 41
Button Amanitas, 32

C

California (state), 40, 111
California Agaricus, 40
California Helvella, 100
Calvatia, description of, 78 (*See* Puffballs)
Calvatia: *caelate*, 91; *craniformis*, 89; *cyathiformis*, 88; *gigantea*, 89
Canary Tricholoma, 76
Cantharellus: *cibarius*, 70; *crispa*, 70
Cascade Mountains, 96, 103
Cauliflower Mushroom, 119
Chanterelles (Cantharellus), description of, 70
Chestnut Bolete, 134
Chicago, 37
Clavariaceae, 119
Clavaria, description of, 110 (*See* Coral and Club Mushrooms)
Clavaria: *amethystina*, 112; *aurea*, 114; *cinerea*, 113; *circinans*, 114; *coralloides*, 112; *cristata*, 115; *fastigiata*, 111; *formosa*, 117; *fusiformis*, 116; *gelatinosa*, 117; *pistillaris*, 118
Clitocybe multiceps, 76
Club Mushrooms, description of, 110
Club-Stemmed Bolete, 130
Cluster Coprinus, 56
Coast Mushroom, 38
Coast Range, 96
Collybia velutipes, 69
Color photographs, listed, 144
Colored Puffball, 93
Commercial Mushrooms, 21, 37
Common Meadow Mushroom (the), 36
Common Meadow or Field Mushrooms, description of, 32 ff.
Cone-Shaped Morel, 96
Coos Bay, Oregon, 111
Coprinus, description of, 46 (*See* Inky Caps)
Coprinus: *atramentarius*, 52; *cinereus*, 56; *comatus*, 50; *fimetarius*, 54; *macrorhiza*, 56; *macrosporus*, 53; *micaceus*, 57; *ovatus*, 51; *pullatus*, 56
Coral Hydnum, 143

Coral Mushrooms, description of, 110
Cranium Puffball, 89
Crater Lake, 111, 131
Crater Lake National Park, 128
Crested Coral (the), 115
Crested Corals, 110
Cup (volva), 21
Cup-Shaped Puffball, 88
Curled Helvella, 105
Curtis Puffball, 85

D

Danger Signals, 21, 120
Deadly Amanita, 16
Death Angel, 16
Death Cup, 17
Delicious Lactarius, 60
Destroying Angel, 19, 27
Drying Mushrooms, 184
Dunghill Mushroom, 54; varieties of, 56
Dwarf Puffball, 93

E

Egg-Yolk Mushroom, 109
Elephant Ears, 108
Etched Puffball, 91
Europe, Europeans, 21, 44, 45, 53, 55, 90, 94, 111, 112, 113
European Amanita, 19
Excellent Puffball, 84

F

Fairy-Ring Mushroom, description of, 44; in folklore, 44; digestibility of, 45
Fairy Rings, 31
False Morel (the), 107
False Morels, description of, 100
Field Mushrooms, description of, 32 ff.
Flat-Cap Mushroom, 43
Fleshy-Pore Mushrooms, description of, 120
Fly Amanita, 18
Folklore, 44
Freezing Mushrooms, 185

G

Gathering, advice on, x, 16
Gelatinous Coral, 117

Gemmed Puffball, 85
Germany, 111
Giant Panaeolus, 58
Giant Puffball, 89
Gilled Mushrooms, 12 ff.
Glossary of terms, 190
"Goat's Beard," 111
Golden Coral, 114
Gray Coral, 113
Green-Gilled Lepiota, 30
Gyromitra, description of, 100 (See False Morels)
Gyromitra: brunnea, 108; esculenta, 106

H

Half-Free Morel, 98
Hedgehog Mushrooms, 140
Helvella, description of, 100, 107 (See False Morels)
Helvella: californica, 100, 104; crispa, 105; infula, 107; lacunosa, 103
Helvellaceae, 94, 100, 106
Hen-of-the-Woods, 138
Honey Mushroom, 67
Horse Mushroom, 41
Hydnums, description of, 140 (See Spine Mushrooms)
Hydnum: caput-medusae, 142; coralloides, 143; erinaceum, 140

I

Identification, viii
Inky Cap (the), 52
Inky Caps, description of, 46; pioneer writing fluid, 46
Inky Egg, 51

K

King Bolete, 129

L

Lactarius, description of, 60
Lactarius deliciosus, 60
Large-Root Coprinus, 56
Large-Spored Coprinus, 53
Leotia lubrica, 104
Lepiota, description of, 22; comparison with Amanitas, 22, 26, 28
Lepiota: americana, 29; molybdites, 30; naucina, 26; procera, 28
Little Chink Puffball, 81

Little Foot Puffball, 82
Little War Clubs, 118
Lycoperdon, description of, 78 (*See* Puffballs)
Lycoperdon: *acuminatum*, 93; *cepaesforme*, 87; *coloratum*, 93; *curtisii*, 85; *eximium*, 84; *gemmatum*, 85; *glabellum*, 83; *pedicellatum*, 82; *pusillum*, 93; *pyriforme*, 86; *rimulatum*, 81; *turneri*, 93

M

Many-Headed Clitocybe, 76
Marasmius oreades, 44
Marketing, 21, 37
Masked Tricholoma, 72
Meadow Mushroom (the), 36
Meadow Mushrooms, description of, 32 ff.; stages of growth, 32; reference to, 44; types of, 32
Medusa's Head, 42
Mica-Cap Coprinus, 57
Milk Mushrooms, description of, 60
Milk Test, 16
Mitrula vitellina, 109
Morchella, description of, 94 (*See* Sponge Mushrooms)
Morchella: *conica*, 96; *esculenta*, 96, 97; *semilibera*, 98
Morels, description of, 94
Mount Hood, 103, 119, 131
Mount Hood National Forest, 128
Mount Jefferson, 103, 131
Mushroom cellars, 37
Mushrooms: origin of word, vii; identifying, viii; parts of, ix, 190; poisoning, x, xi, 12 ff.; size and shape, vi; kinds of—gilled, 12 ff.; without gills, 78 ff.; as food, 161 ff.; selection and preparation for cooking, 161; color change with wounds, bruises, cuts, 39, 40, 120; in survival, 186

N

Naked spores, 100
New York, 37

O

Olympic National Forest, 119
Onion Puffball, 87
Orange Delicious (Delight), 60

Oregon, 27, 38, 40, 43, 94, 103, 111, 119, 128, 140
Oyster Mushroom, 62

P

Pacific Coast (Slope), 19, 22, 39, 94, 97, 110
Pacific Northwest, 32, 37, 94, 105, 118, 120, 125
Panaeolus solidipes, 58
Parasol Mushroom (the), 28
Parasol Mushrooms, description of, 22 ff.; comparison with Amanitas, 22, 26, 27, 28
Pear-Shaped Puffball, 86
Peeling, 37
Phalin, 18
Philadelphia, 37, 45
"Pink Bottom," 36
Pioneer ink, 46
Pits, 94
Pleurotus ostreatus, 62
Pointed Puffball, 93
Poisonous Mushrooms, x, xi, 12 ff., 188 (*See* Amanitas)
Polypores, description of, 120
Polyporus: *frondosus*, 138; *sulphureus*, 137
Pore Mushrooms, description of, 120
Pores, 120
Puffballs, description of, 78

R

Rainier National Forest, 119
Recipes: special, 164 ff.; general, 170 ff.; drying, 184; freezing, 185
Red-Fleshed Agaricus, 39
Red-Stemmed Bolete, 132
Rodman's Mushroom, 37
Rough-Stem Bolete, 125
Round Coral, 114
Rusty Bolete, 128

S

Sac fungi, 100, 104
Saddle-Shaped Helvella, 107
Saint Louis, 37
Salmon River, Oregon, 103
Satyr's Beard, 140
Scotch Bonnets, 45

Shaggy-Mane, 50
Shelf Mushrooms, 137
Silver spoon test, 16
Skull Puffball, 89
Slate Helvella, 103
Slippery Leotia, 104
Smooth Puffball, 83
Sparassis radicata, 119
Spindle Coral, 116
Spine Mushrooms, 140
Sponge Mushroom (the), 97
Sponge Mushrooms, description of, 94
Spore prints, 15
Spores, 15, 78, 110, 120, 140
Sticky-Cap Bolete, 126
Sticky-Stem Bolete, 127
"Stomach fungi," 78
Sulphur Polypore, 137
Survival, 186 ff.

T

Tests, 16, 27
Thick-Footed Bolete, 136
Toadstools, 20, 21
Toasting test, 27
Tooth Mushrooms, 140
Tricholomas (*Tricholoma*), description of, 72
Tricholoma: equestre, 76; *personatum*, 72
True Morels, description of, 94
True Pore Mushrooms, 120

Tube-bearing mushrooms, 120
Turner's Puffball, 93
Two-Colored Bolete, 131

U

Umbrella Mushroom, 22
United States, 21, 36, 37, 53, 55, 107, 113

V

Velvet-Stemmed Collybia, 69

W

Washington (state), 38, 40, 43, 94, 103, 111, 119, 128
West Coast, 37
White-Cap Bolete, 133
White Coral, 112
White Lepiota, 26
Willamette Valley, 27
Wood-Growing Mushrooms, 62

Y

Yellow-Cap Bolete, 129
Yellow Chanterelle, 70
Yellow Coral, 111
Yellow-Flesh Bolete, 127
Yellow-Tipped Coral, 117
Yellow Tricholoma, 76